AF539804

ESSAYS ON TEACHING SCIENCE

Books by **Marlow Ediger** *and*
Digumarti Bhaskara Rao

Administration of Schools
Community Colleges
Curriculum Organisation
Curriculum of School Subjects
Effective Schooling
Effective School Curriculum
Elementary Curriculum
Elementary Curriculum Improvement
Essays on Teaching Mathematics
Essays on Teaching Science
Essays on Teaching Social Studies
Essays on Teaching Reading
Essays on Teaching and Learning
Improving School Administration
Issues in School Curriculum
Language Arts Curriculum
Philosophy and Curriculum
Psychology and Curriculum
Quality School Education
Reading Curriculum and Instruction
Relevancy in Elementary Curriculum
School Organisation
School Curriculum and Administration
Science Curriculum
Teaching English Successfully
Teaching Language Arts Successfully
Teaching Mathematics Successfully
Teaching Science Successfully
Teaching Social Studies Successfully
Teaching Mathematics in Elementary Schools
Teaching Science in Elementary Schools
Successful School Administration
Successful School Education

published by
Discovery Publishing House

ESSAYS ON TEACHING SCIENCE

by

Dr. MARLOW EDIGER
Emeritus Professor of Education
Truman State University
P.O. Box 417, 201 W 22nd St
North Newton KS 67117
United States of America

and

Dr. DIGUMARTI BHASKARA RAO
Reader and Research Director
R.V.R. College of Education
D-43 (277) S.V.N. Colony
Guntur-522006, India

DISCOVERY PUBLISHING HOUSE PVT. LTD.
NEW DELHI-110 002

Published by:
Tilak Wasan

DISCOVERY PUBLISHING HOUSE PVT. LTD.
4831/24, Prahlad Street, Ansari Road
Darya Ganj, New Delhi-110002 (India)
Phone: +91-11-23279245, 43764432
Fax: +91-11-23253475
E-mail: parul.wasan@gmail.com
discoverypublishinghouse@gmail.com
info@discoverypublishinggroup.com
web: www.discoverypublishinggroup.com

***First Edition:* 2011**
ISBN: 978-81-8356-882-1

Essays on Teaching Science

Printed at:
Shree Balaji Art Press
Delhi

dedicated
to

Prof. V. Sudhakar
The University of English and Foreign Languages
Hyderabad - 500007
&
Member
Southern Regional Committee
National Council for Teacher Education
Bangalore

in
recognition
of his
excellent achievements
in the field of Education

Preface

Science is a systematic enterprise of gathering knowledge about nature and organizing and condensing that knowledge into testable laws and theories. As knowledge has increased, some methods have proved more reliable than others, and today the scientific method is the standard for science. It includes the use of careful observation, experimentation, measurement, mathematics, and replication to be considered a science. Now the teaching of science is made a school subject across the world and such subject needs successful teaching.

In the successful teaching of science, the infrastructure, the equipment, the administrator, the teacher, the curriculum, the library, the science laboratory, the academic atmosphere, the teaching-learning programmes, etc., play their legitimate role.

This book will be of great use to curriculum designers and teachers and administrators.

Digumarti Bhaskara Rao
digumartibhaskararao@redeiffmail.com

Sri Sai Soudha
D-43 S.V.N. Colony
Guntur 522006
India

Contents

Preface

1. Science for All Pupils in the School Curriculum 1
2. Meaning in Science Curriculum 8
3. Current Events in Ongoing Science Lessons and Units of Study 14
4. Revisiting the Concepts of Scope and Sequence in Science 18
5. Leadership in Science Curriculum 23
6. Teaching Science and English Language Learners ... 29
7. Methods of Teaching Science 35
8. Teaching of Science 41
9. Readiness for Learning in Science 44
10. Parent/Teacher Conferences and Science Curriculum 52
11. Poetry in Science Curriculum 57
12. Constructivism and Science Curriculum 63
13. Developings Student Interest in Science 73
14. Establishing Meaning in Science Curriculum 79
15. Assessment of Student Achievement in Science 87
16. Motivating Student Learning in Science 93
17. New Science Teacher in School Setting 100
18. Mentoring and Science Teacher 107
19. Substitute Teacher in Science 113

20. Assessting in Science Using Teacher Observation 117
21. Portfolios in Science 123
22. A Stimulating Science Vocabulary Environment 128
23. Oral Communication in Science Lessons and Units of Study 134
24. Pupil, Writing and Science Curriculum 142
25. Integrated Science Curriclum 148
26. Children's Literature and Science Curriclum 154
27. Reading Comprehension in Science Curriculum 159
28. Pre-student Teaching Field Experiences 164
29. Science Fairs and Student 170
30. Leadership to Improve Science Curriculum 175
31. School Principal as Science Supervisor 182
32. Decision-making in Science Curriculum 191
33. Psychology of Learning and Science Curriculum 196
34. Motivating Students in Science Curriculum 203
35. Data Driven Decision-making in Science 209
36. Readiness for Learning in Science 216
Additional Reading 224
Index 249

1

Science for All Pupils in the School Curriculum

Individual live in a scientific world. Science has brought tremendous achievements for the human condition such as continual improvement in medical practices, manual labour saving devices, transportation, communication, and safety in food products consumed, among others. The natural world may create havocs such as earthquakes, mud slides, floods, ice storms, drought, tornados/hurricanes, soil erosion, and hail. The latter ruin farm crops and cause heavy expenses for building repairs, in general. It has been difficult to deal with losses from these affects, but human beings need to rebuild and redo while attempting to minimize causes for these losses. Vital needed improvements include having underground cable to avoid electrical problems from ice storms; people do depend upon electricity for heat and survival in homes across the nation. Other salient needs include :

- quality health care available to all in society, regardless of income levels
- safe, updated school buildings with good teachers for each pupil

- road and bridge repairs for safety in travel and transportation
- federal moneys available to assist students to go to and graduate from college or technical school
- safe, affordable housing for each person
- job market which has necessary work with adequate salaries for workers
- mass transit system providing transportation at a reasonable cost to individuals (Ediger, 2008).

In each of the above situations and ideals, science has an important role to play which makes it a necessity to provide a quality science curriculum for each pupil. A starting point here would be to evaluate - if science instruction is receiving its fair share of school time. Adequate time is needed to provide for an effective science curriculum. To use the allotted time efficiently, pupils must experience vital objectives to achieve, be it mandated or locally developed. The following objectives are highly important to achieve by pupils :

- objective, careful observers of science phenomenon
- critical and creative thinking abilities, as well as problem-solving skills
- metacognition skills to reflect upon what has been learned
- doing quality projects, evaluated in terms of desired criteria
- being able to carryout science experiments to evaluate information
- showing learnings acquired through graphs, charts, and tables
- reading science content with meaning and understanding
- listening with a variety of purposes involved (Parker, 2001).

The list could go on to include using inferential thinking, and developing good attitudes toward science learnings in general, such as pupils being curious pertaining to the natural environment. Updating teacher knowledge and skills is a continuous concern. Each school needs to possess a library for teachers to house teacher education science textbooks and journals, as well as a reputable daily newspaper/news-magazine which contain accounts on current events involving noteworthy science happenings (floods and tornados, for example). There should be a table and comfortable chairs, suitable for reading activities. Science teachers need to be encouraged to use the science library to promote inservice growth (Zales and Linger, 2008).

Also, teachers should be challenged to take graduate courses in science eduction. Taking courses online or at an approved university increases chances for teacher growth in teaching science. There are always possibilities of doing an independent study in providing for pupil individual differences in teaching learners. The point remains that science education needs to be emphasized.

Grade level teacher discussion groups should be held to share ideas on improving instruction. New ideas for teaching may be tried out in the classroom and results reported back to the discussion group. From these diverse inservice education approaches, teachers may wish to provide suggestions for a quality workshop whereby all participants benefit from its proceedings. Thus, a theme might be chosen and a large group session held to select problem areas in science teaching. From these identified problem areas, committees may be formed to work in the direction of solving respective problems n science instruction. Suggestions for teaching an innovation should provide opportunities for teaching science in the classroom. Participants at the workshop need to be informed of these outcomes. One salient area of instruction is in doing science experiments safely in the classroom. One variable alone needs to be tested in an experiment for pupils. The carefully designed experiment needs to stress an hypothesis to be tested. As a result of testing, the hypothesis may be modified, revised, or left as is. The methods of science must be stressed in experimentation. Teachers need to appraise the quality of the workshop in terms of desired criteria such as

- was the workshop beneficial to improve instruction?
- did you try out innovative ideas in your classroom?
- how did pupils in your classroom benefit from the ideals emphasized in the workshop?
- did you feel free to ask questions of consultants in the workshop? (National Science Education Standards, 1996).

Evaluation results may be tabulated and used for future inservice education endeavours. The purpose of workshops is to assist teachers to provide quality objectives, learning opportunities, and evaluation procedures in teaching and learning situations. The science curriculum must be assessed and updated periodically. Pupils individually need to achieve as much as possible in science. Individual differences must be provided for.

Demonstration teaching is another facet and procedure of curriculum improvement in science. Who might do the demonstration teaching? Attempts must be made to identify science teachers, presently teaching or retirees, to do quality demonstration teaching in science. Science education professors from a nearby university may be willing to demonstrate how to teach selected concepts and generalizations in science. Carefully chosen video-tapes, also, might well provide models for science teaching. Methods stressed should assist pupils of all achievement levels to attain vital objectives of instruction. The point is that there are a plethora of ways to improve science teaching. The science supervisor, too, needs to appraise teaching quality in the classroom in order to help pupils attain more optimally. He/she may assess science teachers in the following areas:

- providing meaningful learning activities so that pupils understand what was taught
- engaging pupils in ongoing activities and experiences to encourage interest in learning
- assisting pupils to perceive purpose in ongoing science lessons and units of study
- encouraging pupil curiosity in science
- helping pupils to reflect upon what was learned to emphasize retention of learnings acquired
- guiding pupils to use the internet to extend achieved learnings (Smolleck, 2007).

To aid pupils in reading science content, such as from the basal textbook, the teacher needs to assist pupils in securing background information for the ensuing activity. Thus, the science teacher needs to discuss relevant illustrations directly related to the subject matter to be read. Questions raised here, by pupils, might well be answered during/from the reading experience. Prior to reading, pupils need to see the new words, enlarged on a screen, projected from a computer. Each word must be highlighted as it is being identified. Meaning must be attached to each word as used in context in the basal textbook in science. Pupils should then be able to comprehend ideas in context. Followup experiences from textbook reading might include

- discussing answers to questions indepth
- identifying a problem area and finding a related solution
- doing a mural or diorama
- constructing a model
- working cooperatively on a project
- writing a report of major ideas read.

The basal textbook activity may be extended by having pupils read for information on additional self selected science content. Thus, the science teacher may choose library books to be housed at a learning center in the classroom. The library books are on different topics in science and are at diverse reading levels to provide for individual learners. Each pupil may choose a library book to read. Decision making is then involved. During the silent reading time, the science teacher may ask pupils individually a few questions along the way to assess comprehension and time on task. Assistance also must be provided to pupils who need help in word recognition. The reading experience needs to flow as seamless as possible in order that pupils might gain vital facts, concepts, and generalizations in science (Rice, 2002).

IN CLOSING

Time needs to be used wisely in teaching science. Pupils need to achieve worthwhile objectives in each unit of study. However, pupils do need time to reflect upon what has been learned indepth. Pertaining to wasted school time, Olson (2008) wrote :

> Some procedures will always be necessary, but many can be streamlined or omitted. Transitions between rooms, subjects, and breaks are prime spots where time can be saved. Get students started quickly when they return to the room. Take attendance while students are working on an academic task. When possible, show relevant clips of videos rather than the entire program. Have smooth procedures for collecting and distributing paperwork. Decide if "free time" or "homework time" at the end of the day is worth the cost to your science programs. Evan a few minutes add up to a significant amount of time over the course of the school year.

REFERENCES

Ediger, Marlow and D. Bhaskara Rao (2007), *School Science Education.* New Delhi, India: Discovery Publishing House.

Ediger, Marlow (2008), "The School and Students in Society," *Journal of Instructional Psychology,* 35 (3), 260-264.

National Science Education Standards (1996), Washington, DC: National Research Council (NRC).

National Science Teachers Association (2009), *NSTA Reports.* Arlington, Virginia: The Association.

Olson, Joanne K. (2008), "Methods and Strategies," *Science and Children,* 46 (3), 52-53.

Parker, Walter (2001), *Social Studies in Elementary Education.* Upper Saddle River, New Jersey: Prentice, Hall, Inc.

Rice, D.C. (2002), "Using Trade Books in Teaching Elementary School Science," *The Reading Teacher,* 55 (6), 552-565.

Smolleck, L.D. (2007), Science in the Elementary School Classroom-Post NCLB," *Teachers College Record.*

Zales, Charlotte Rappe, and Connie S. Unger (2008), "The Science and Literacy Framework", *Science and Children,* 46(3), 42-45.

2

Meaning in Science Curriculum

The science teacher has a salient responsibility in assisting pupils to develop meaningful learnings. Too frequently, quickly covering the contents in a basal textbook is stressed without making certain that learners understand what is taught. Pupils need to attach meaning to each concept and generalization taught. Otherwise, pupils will be hindered in understanding subsequent subject matter. An important strategy in teaching is to help pupils attain adequate background information before proceeding with new objectives of instruction. Background information may be secured with the use of authentic content, vicarious experiences, and printed materials. Pupils need to experience developmentally appropriate learning opportunities in order to achieve, accomplish, and grow.

Meaning, Teaching, and Learning in Science

Background information, activated with teacher assistance, needs to relate to previous learner experiences. Thus, the pupil connects the old with the new science subject matter. This connection is vital in order to attach meaning to ongoing facts, concepts, and generalizations in each lessons and unit of study. Sequence resides in the minds of pupils and must be planned within this framework. To activate background knowledge, the teacher needs to help pupils to review previously acquired ideas. Thus if pupils are studying Animals with Backbones, they may experience a review of amphibians, going through the stages of egg, tadpoles, and the adult state of frog. This can be experienced through illustrations, printouts from the computer, and power point presentations. Learners must feel free to ask questions and obtain answers to fill gaps in knowledge (Ediger and Rao, 2007).

To connect with the new subject-matter, pupils might well be studying how frogs are a part of the ecology in the natural environment. Interaction with other amphibians and animals with/without backbones, as well as plant life must be studied. Indepth learning emphasizes that the teacher use a variety of kinds of concrete, semi-concrete, as well as abstract activities. In this way, pupils may attach meaning to ongoing experiences.

Also to achieve new objectives, pupils must perceive purpose in learning. Reasons are then accepted for achieving/ learning new subject-matter. Pupils, in many situations, do not learn effectively due to having a lack of purpose. The teacher may state and elaborate on the purpose such as, "Today we are going to study some possible reasons for the frog population dwindling in numbers and how this affects the environment." Pupils may also hypothesize why it is poignant to learn about frogs and other animals in the ecological setting. Intrinsically, pupils may then perceive reasons for wholehearted invovlement. Terminology must be used which pupils understand. Meaning theory is always salient in teaching and learning situations. It assists pupils to achieve new, related objectives of instruction; otherwise, pupils might become bored with a lack of challenge. Or, learners may be frustrated if the new learnings are too advanced and unrelated to those acquired previously (Jackson, *et al.*, 2008).

Interest factors in learning assist pupils to accept reasons for participating wholeheartedly in ongoing science lessons and units of study. Stimulating methods of having pupils learn by discovery can be exciting. This is opposite of being told or lectured on subject-matter to be learned. There are science teachers who use a seamless learning by discovery procedure of instruction. At a National Science Teachers Association convention, a high school physics instructor remarked that he never responded with answers to questions, raised by students. Instead, he lead them to correct answers with a series of ordered questions. Thinking is a major objective here (Ritchart and Perkins, 2008).

Interest is also encouraged within engaging learning opportunities. A classroom which emphasizes continuous learning is salient such as in the late spring months having a jar of eggs/tadpoles swimming in water for pupil observation. As these are observed, pupils ask questions of each other and of the teacher pertaining to the phenomenon involved. The identified questions set the stage for problem solving. Different reference sources may be used to secure necessary information. Committees might be formed to attain information with the science teacher serving as a guide and helper. Each committee needs to respect contributions from its members, stay on the topic being pursued, keep the activity moving forward, develop conclusions, and present its findings to other committees. Findings may be shown with the project method whereby a product is completed, which meet the following standards :

- careful planning of the project
- all committee members being actively involved in doing the project
- neatness in the final pursued project.

The writer when supervising university student teachers observed many pupils who truly were interested in the project method and attained major science concepts and generalizations as well as being able to work together. They appeared to work together well in an atmosphere of respect. Pupils tend to understand science subject matter with a hands on approach much better than a lecture/heavy explanation approach (Dewey, 1916).

Frogs, as well as other vertebrates, live in an environment which includes plant life. To show how significant sunlight is to different plants, the teacher may provide spinach seeds to be seeded properly in small pots. The seed is the same kind for each of two pots with similar soil, as well as needed moisture. One pot receives adequate sunshine after the plants appear above ground; the other is covered with a paper sack. Pupils may then hypothesize and check the hypothesis by observing how appropriate sunlight affects plant growth. The experiment may be replicated if necessary. The amount of moisture might also be checked as a variable in promoting plant growth, with all other conditions kept constant including quality of seed, sunlight, and soil. Experiments conducted need to be on the understanding level of learners so that meaningful learnings accrue. They must be clearly visible to all participants. Careful observations, here, by pupils is salient. Hypotheses need to be recorded in order to test each (American Association for the Advancement of Science, 1989).

Pupils need to be able to read well from basal science textbooks, internet sources, as well as library books among others; selected hypotheses might well be checked through reading. Meaningful reading might be achieved, using the following recommended methodology, with pupils developing/using :

- context clues to ascertain unknown words in context
- analytical procedures in word recognition such as phonetic analysis, syllabication skills, and dividing a word into prefixes, and suffixes
- main ideas, subordinate content, and details, related, in reading science subject-matter

- critical reading (separating facts from opinions, fantasy from reality, as well as accurate from inaccurate statements), creative reading (developing new, original ideas and ways of pursing a goal), and problem solve.
- evaluative procedures in appraising the worth of subject matter read for purposeful activities (National Research Council, 1996).

Current Events in Science Units and Lessons

With a quality current events programme, the teacher develops and maintains an updated science programme. There are a plethora of current happenings which affect people around the world. Pupils must understand why these happenings occur in nature. Causes and effects need to be studied. Meaning needs to be attached to these learnings. Common occurrences in natural disasters include the following and need to be included in a developmental current events curriculum in science :

- floods, mud slides, and soil erosion
- tornados and hurricanes which also cause heavy property loss
- volcanic eruptions
- forest fires, draught, and water shortages.

Pupils need to study each of the above meaningfully and understand what can be done to alleviate human suffering from these occurrences. Diverse organizations and volunteers which provide assistance must be studied.

There are numerous things done to make for a cleaner environment as well as save energy costs. These include :

- use of wind energy such as windmills
- utilization of solar energy including solar panels on homes

- updating appliances to make for more energy efficiency
- use of ethanol instead of gasoline and diesel fuel to power vehicles
- insulating houses to preserve energy used in summer and winter
- having plants indoors to minimize the effects of carbon dioxide (Ediger, 2009).

Pupils must understand why it is salient to conserve energy and how each of the above assists in conservation methods as well as provide for a cleaner environment. The list may well be extended by pupils with teacher guidance. Direct observation should be made by pupils of these endeavors, whenever possible.

REFERENCES

American Association for the Advancement of Science (1989), *Benchmarks for Science Literacy*. New York: Oxford University Press.

Dewey, John (1916), *Democracy and Education*. New York: Macmillan Company.

Ediger, Marlow (2009), "Innovations in Teaching Science," *Connecticut Journal of Science Education*, 47 (2), 27-28.

Ediger, Marlow, and D. Bhaskara Rao (2007), *School Science Education*. New Delhi, India : Discovery Publishing House.

Jackson, Julie, *et al.*, (2008), "Connections Charts and Book Talk Groups," *Science and Children*, 46 (3), 27-31.

National Research Council (1996), *National Science Education Standards*. Washington, DC : National Academy Press.

Ritchhart, Ron, and David Perkins (2008), "Making Thinking Visible," *Educational Leadership*, 65 (5), 57-63.

3

Current Events in Ongoing Science Lessons and Units of Study

Current events in science assist pupils to stay abreast of today's happenings. In a democracy it is very salient for all to be well-informed of transpiring events. Science in the news helps pupils to understand what is happening in local, State, national, and international events. Pupils need to connect with these happenings as well as attach meaning to diverse occurrences. Ill-informed persons lose out on how science is involved in current events. The science teacher must guide learners to perceive purpose in vital happenings which transpire. Reasons then exist for indepth learning into causes of current happenings on the planet earth. Most current events items deal with the natural environment. These include the following natural disasters :

- mudslides which may devour entire villages and cities
- forest fires caused by lightning and other natural occurrences which destroy an entire area of farm crops, homes, and other buildings
- earthquakes which weaken or demolish villages, huts and stronger buildings, roads and bridges
- volcanic eruptions which bury what is in its way and cause panic

- hail which weakens or eliminates agricultural production as well as causes severe losses/damage to different kinds of structures
- tornados which can wipe out a complete city as well as wind power to lift huge trucks into the air
- tsunamis with it destructible force of flood waters following an underwater earthquake.

Learning Opportunities

To understand each of the above asterisked current events items, pupils need to experience a variety of developmentally appropriate activities. Each happing needs to be pin-pointed on a map and globe. Thus, print-outs of illustrations from the internet need to be in the offing for study. Additional illustrations to be discussed in depth might well come from the following reference sources :

- a power point presentations showing a sequence of happenings as in a mudslide
- pictures from a basal science textbook indicating destructive forces of forest fires
- illustrations from science encyclopedias on faults, folding, and earthquakes
- teacher and pupil made models pertaining to volcanos
- newspaper illustrations and accounts of hail and its effects on farm crops and buildings
- scenes from newsmagazines showing the power of hurricanes, tornados, and cyclones
- listening to TV and radio news accounts on the effect of tsunamis in different regions.

There are several methods to emphasize in organizing the science current events program. One approach is to relate the happening to an ongoing science unit of study. This has its merits since it integrates and indicates relationships of what is being studied. This procedure views subject-matter holistically, not in separate parts. Pupils tend to remember content studied better if the new learnings are related to those previously studied. Sequence is then in evidence and resides in the minds of learners. The science teacher might then ascertain at which point in the science curriculum it would be best for current events instruction. In a science unit on "The Changing Surface of the Earth," the concept of *mudslides* may be stressed at the time this concept is being studied. There is then a gradual transition from what is generally taught in the science unit to incorporating the new learning.

A second procedure in teaching science current event is to bring the happening for attention, regardless of it relationship to an ongoing science unit of study. This is done when a relevant happening is unrelated to what is presently being studied in a science unit of study. There are a plethora of current happenings which are unrelated to the present science unit of study being emphasized. Relevancy in the news then indicates there is a need, for example, to report on *forest fires* even though the present unit of study cannot be related to that concept.

Third, the current events concept may be unrelated to the current unit being studied, but may be broadened to become an entire science unit of study. Thus the concept *earthquakes* may be highly important in the news since many regions are experiencing this science phenomena in different, salient locations on the planet earth. It takes time and quality teaching to assist pupils to understand earthquakes and their after effects in depth. Objectives, learning opportunities, and evaluation procedures may then be developed to teach a developmentally appropriate science unit of study, based on a vital current happening.

Fourth, the integrated current events unit of study may be taught emphasizing science as an academic area largely. Thus in a unit on *hurricanes and tornados,* the following academic disciplines in science may be stressed: earth sciences, physics with its resulting forces in bringing about destructive effects, and biology with its effects on plants and animals. To integrate science and current events with the social studies, among other academic disciplines, the following emphases may be included :

- aid and assistance provided by different relief agencies to minimize pain and suffering
- the history of major major hurricanes on the planet earth and why they occur
- geographical regions where major hurricanes and tornados transpired
- assistance provided from different private and governmental agencies to clean up and rebuild an area.

A quality science current events program advocates that teachers follow selected criteria to optimize pupil learning. Thus, pupils need to :

- attach meaning and understanding pertaining to teaching and learning situations
- be actively involved in learning and participate fully in discussing science current events items
- perceive purpose in being engaged in achieving vital objectives
- experience intrinsic sequence as well as perceive subject matter as being related
- do critical and creative thinking as well as problem solving.

In closing, pupils must experience quality objectives, engaging learning opportunities for pupils to achieve these objectives, and valid/reliable evaluation procedures to notice learner progress.

4

Revisiting the Concepts of Scope and Sequence in Science

Two highly valuable concepts to consider in science instruction are scope (what should be taught) and sequence (when should these be brought into teaching and learning situations). Science lesson plans and units of study must reflect the saliency of these two concepts.

Scope in Science Teaching

The objectives of instruction will indicate the totality of science subject-matter and skills to be taught. There is much to incorporate in any unit of study. Thus, the scope must receive careful consideration in terms of that which is relevant. Which understandings and abilities should the science teacher emphasize, for example, in a unit on "The Changing Surface of the Earth?" The science teacher, after much planning, might well consider content such as the following :

- active volcanos and how they make for changes in geology/geography
- the formation of igneous, sedimentary, and metamorphic rocks

- fossil information providing subject matter dealing with the history and evolution of the planet earth
- mudslides, floods, erosion, tornados, hurricanes, among others (Ediger, 2007).

Each of the above asterisked items may be stated as a general objective or written in measurable terms. How will pupils achieve these objectives? Learning opportunities then must be chosen. Thus, a variety of experiences need provision to provide for different aptitudes, intelligences, and interest differences among learners. Concrete, semi-concrete, and abstract learning activities must be in the offing to meet pupil needs. They may be adapted to the following :

- individual and collective/committee endeavours
- problem-solving and project methods
- construction experiences and audio-visual presentations
- reading of abstract materials
- written work including writing summaries, reports, conclusions, outlines, as well as narratives/ information content
- speaking experiences such as oral and book reports, dramatizations, discussions, peer group presentations, among others
- listening activities in science units of study including power point presentations, DVDs, CDs, as well as those interacting with speaking experiences listed previously above
- art, music, social studies, mathematics, and literature integration as they relate to ongoing lessons
- quality feedback from testing situations (National Research Council, 1996).

The breadth of objectives and experiences provide for scope in the science curriculum. Learning may be maximized in science for pupils by paying careful attention to scope in science. Trivia and the unimportant are then weeded out.

Sequence in Science Learnings

Sequence is highly salient as a topic to discuss. The order of providing learning experiences makes for achievement or a lack thereof. Some guidance for the science teacher might come from a salient rule of starting with the concrete or life like experiences such as experiments in ongoing lessons and units of study. This is followed with the semi-concrete as in a power point presentation whereby pupils perceive illustrations, not reality, of what is being studied as in fish, amphibians, reptiles, birds, and mammals, in a science unit on animals. Rich discussions do occur from the concrete as well as the semi-concrete. These examples should provide needed background information to use in scaffolding in which pupils are ready to achieve higher cognitive level objectives with abstract leanings including reading of science subject matter in particular. The concrete, semi-concrete, and abstract might well include oral communication, listening, and writing skills, as well as related subject matter from other academic disciplines (Eisner, 2006).

Instruction should always be adapted to the learner's present level of achievement. The writer is a firm believer in Vygotsky's Zone of Proximal Development in that encouragement and challenge are possible with good teaching for the learner to extend his/her repertoire of knowledge and skills. Inherent in this statement is the motivation factor whereby the following motivate (provide a higher energy level for learning) :

- develop and maintain pupil interest in a topic our project. Interest is a powerful factor in learning and carries the study of a topic or a project to fruition.
- assist learners to see the relevance or usefulness of science subject matter being considered and studied.

- consider the developmental level of the pupil in the teaching and learning process; scaffold learning to guide learners to higher levels of progress.
- permit pupil input into learning activities and opportunities whereby choices may be made in terms of what to learn.
- help pupils to achieve feelings of belonging; being an isolate violates learner feelings of adequacy.
- guide pupils to be successful achievers within the framework of a challenging science lesson or unit of study.
- meet esteem needs of individuals with honest praise for work well done. Each pupil craves recognition for improved performance (National Science Teachers Association, 2001).

There are a plethora of instructional plans in aiding pupil science achievement. The following may be used entoto or in separate/integrated situations :

- personalizing instruction whereby the science teacher plans learning activities individually with pupils. The experiences are designed to meet personal needs in science instruction.
- learning centers in which pupils, individually, choose from alternative learning opportunities at different centers, each of which contains task cards for assistance in making selections.
- a basics approach whereby pupils are taught sequential learnings using a carefully chosen science textbook. Audio-visual aids, as well as other technology, are utilized to enrich pupil experiences.
- a science curriculum, heavily endowed with the latest in technology such as lap tops, cell phones, iPods, iTunes, science video games, smart phones, white boards, as well as other mobile technology.

Technology might also be integrated with each of the above asterisked plans of instruction (Ediger, 2009).

Within each plan of instruction, pupils might well acquire increasingly complex science subject matter content. Thus, with quality sequence, optimal learner achievement is possible.

IN CLOSING

Science teacher sand supervisors need to pay careful attention to the scope of the curriculum. This involves careful selection of what is taught to minimize the rival band the unimportant. Sequence , a related concept, stresses the science teacher ordering when subject matter is to be emphasized. Good, planned sequence with scaffolding assists pupils to achieve well with instruction related to the developmental ieveis of learners (Brady, 2008).

REFERENCES

Brady, Marion (2008), "Cover the Material or Teach Students to Think?" *Educational Leadership*, 65 *(5)*, 64-67.

Ediger, Marlow (2007), *School Science Education*. New Delhi, India: Discovery Publishing House, Chapter Six.

Ediger, Marlow (2009), "Oral Communication and Science Teaching," *Experiments in Education*, 37(1), 17-20.

Eisner, Elliot (2006),"The Satisfaction of Teaching," *Educational Leadership*, 63 (6), 44-47.

National Research Council (1996), National Science Education Standards. Washington DC: National Science Teachers Association.

National Science Teachers Association (2001), Classroom Assessment and the National Education Standards. Washington DC : NSTA.

5

Leadership in Science Curriculum

Leadership is needed to improve any curriculum area, science included. Here, leaders may come from within the local public school teachers of science. A leader may be designated or a cooperative type of leadership might well emerge. The point being that science teachers must study, evaluate, and modify, if needed, current procedures of instruction. A quality science teacher's library should be available with the latest science teacher's journals as well as textbooks and audio-visual aids, to invigorate the teaching of science. Science teachers need to read subject-matter and discuss related ideas among participants. Relevant ideas must be tried out in the classroom with results of teaching reported to the inservice deduction group. Leadership, then, may focus on the following inservice activities :

- reading and discussing selected ideas from science teaching journals and textbooks
- encouraging members to incorporate in teaching that which meets desired criteria
- reporting to the group how the innovation worked out in the classroom

- video-tape the new approach for purposes of analyzing by the inservice group (Ediger 2003).

Curriculum Development in Science

There are a plethora of additional means of improving science instruction. Growth in science teaching should be ongoing. The inservice group of science teachers must set up a schedule of times for meeting. The topics may be established ahead of time or be open ended, depending upon feelings of participants. The needs of teachers is highly salient. When supervising university student teachers, the writer noticed three important items in conducting an experiment. First, pupils could not see clearly what was transpiring. Thus, selected pupils could not observe the experiment carefully due to seating arrangements or the materials used were not large enough. Second, pupils jumped to hasty conclusions without observing what truly did occur in the experiment, based on evidence. Third, there were too many variables in an experiment without holding all variables constant, except the one being tested. Objectivity in-clarity of thinking is very important in science. Pupils with teacher guidance need to discuss the results of the experiment which involves critical and creative thinking, as well as problem solving. With inservice education, science experiments need to be carefully chosen and relevant to pupils. Inservice education may improve experimentation as a learning activity in ongoing lessons and units of study (Mechta 2010).

Science experiments may be used to initiate, develop, as well as culminate a unit of study. To extend learnings, pupils might well read from a reputable source of information. Depending upon where pupils are in reading achievement and the kind of reference source used, learners may need assistance in the following :

- *Word recognition*. Unknown words may be pronounced by the teacher or a capable reader. Better yet, to have pupils become independent in reading science materials, a pupil may need help with context clues. This approach assists pupils to think of a word which fits in meaningfully with the rest of the sentence or paragraph. Context clues also guide pupils in vocabulary development since the surrounding words will help to ascertain a working definition. Unknown words may be posted on a word wall whereby learners may later rehearse the identification and meaning of these words.

- *Background information.* Learning is based upon what had been acquired previously; the content might be hazy and lack clarity which good teaching may overcome.
- *If basal textbooks* are utilized, the new words may be seen in print on a whiteboard prior to reading subject matter. These words may be discussed so that understanding of content is involved. From discussions related to the illustrations in the basal or brought in by the teacher, problems or questions may be identified for which solutions may be found through the actual reading experience. Extended learnings are also invited whereby pupils with teacher guidance identify a problem, gather information from a variety of reference sources, develop an hypothesis, test the hypothesis, and revise it if need be with critical and creative thinking (Dryfoos 2008).

A project method may also be used to encourage pupil interest. The project might well involve a construction activity. Here, pupils with teacher guidance in.an ongoing science unit may decide upon a model to be made. There are myriad models which may be constructed. Thus, pupils might be curious about developing a solar collector. Once the purpose is established, then plans must be made for its fruition. Information from a variety of reference sources need to be gathered including the internet and computer sources. Relevant information must be acquired to fulfil the purpose.

Evaluation of what is salient needs to be sorted from that which lacks saliency. Thus, much content might well be acquired, but what is relevant needs to be selected. After the planning has been completed, then the actual execution of these need to be incorporated as learning experiences. These learning activities need to emphasize completeness, neatness, and conscientious work (Darling-Hammond 1998).

Committee work may be stressed in developing the project. Criteria for doing quality small grow endeavors need to be stressed. Thus, the following are significant :

- each participate optimally, but no one dominating the committee
- members working for the good of developing a quality project
- individuals not participating wholeheartedly need encouragement and motivation to achieve. Each member of the committee is appraised in terms of effort put forth
- good human relations is emphasized in the learning experience; quality attitudes are of utmost importance (National Research Council, 2001).

Library Books to Expand Science Learnings

Science library books need to be ample in number for each unit of study. They need to be on diverse categories such as those dealing with biology, chemistry, earth science, and the environment. Pupils with teacher guidance might then select sequential books on their reading levels. With scaffolding of ideas contained in library books, the science teacher might well assist pupils to achieve at a hinger level than would ordinarily be the case. Challenge and positive achievement are two major concepts to emphasize in teaching and learning situations (Pearman, 2008).

The contents of each library book may be used in discussions as these related science units are taught.

Enjoyment in reading science materials also must be in the offing. This becomes a motivator for increased learner achievement. In addition to using library book content in discussions, they might well be also utilized in the following ways :

- in sustained silent reading (SSR) whereby special time is devoted to choice of reading materials for pupils to read silently to themselves
- in individualized reading in which the self selected reading material is discussed with the teacher at the end of that selection. The teacher may notice pupil comprehension and understanding of science subject matter as well as oral reading skills
- in the teacher reading orally to pupils during story hour
- in peer discussion groups whereby participants assist each other with scaffolding of ideas (Ediger 2007).

Skills for Science Teachers and Inservice Education

To become proficient participants within the framework of inservice education, science teachers need to collaborate. This involves cooperation, acceptance, and harmonious relationships. Trust must be developed among participants to work toward the goal of improving the curriculum. Collaboration involves dialogue. Dialogue emphasizes communicating with each other with clarity, meaning, and respect. Rudeness and intimidation have no roles to play in furthering the presenting of ideas relevant to the improvement of teaching and learning situations. There are a plethora of inservice education situations whereby collaboration and dialogue are needed as in the following :

- constructivism versus behaviourism
- small group endeavours versus individual activities
- cooperation versus competition
- depth versus breadth in ongoing science lessons and units of study

- locally selected objectives versus mandated objectives
- portfolios versus testing to ascertain learner achievement and progress (Tompkins 2006).

Each of the above-asterisked items needs thorough discussion in order to facilitate modifying science instruction where necessary. The focal point must be upon the learner in determining what is best.

REFERENCES

Darling-Hammond, L. (1998), "Teachers and Teaching," *Educational Researcher,* 27(1), 5-15.

Dryfoos, Joy G. (2008), "Centers of Hope," *Educational Leadership,* 65 (7), 38-43.

Ediger, Marlow (2002), *Teaching Science Successfully.* New Delhi, India: Discovery Publishing House, Chapter Six.

Ediger, Marlow (2007), *Schol Science Education*, New Delhi, India: Discover Publishing House.

Mechta, Meenakshi (2010), "Personality Needs and Academic Achievement of Sr. Secondary Students," *Edutracks*, 8 (7), 27-30. Printed in India.

National Research Council (2001), *National Science Education Standards for Schools*, Washington, DC: National Science Teachers Association.

Pearman, Cathy, 2008), "Independent Reading of CD-ROM Storybooks," 61 (8), 594-603.

Tompkins, G. E. (2006), *Literacy for the 21st Century: A Balanced Approach.* Upper Saddle River, New Jersey: Pearson Prentice Hall.

6

Teaching Science and English Language Learners

With the increase in English Language Learners (ELL) in the public schools, it behooves professional teachers to update skills in teaching. This includes the science curriculum which is pinpointed in this manuscript. ELL pupils come from homes where English is not spoken at all or is not the dominant language. States have requirements here as to who to include as ELL learners. There are criteria for teachers to use in teaching science to this category of pupils in order to optimize learning :

- subject-matter must be meaningful so that pupils understand what is taught
- interest is learning is vital and is inherent if learning is to occur
- purpose in learning is highly significant; otherwise pupils may not perceive value in achieving objectives within ongoing lessons and units in science
- learning styles vary within learners in terms of how science is taught
- individual differences must be provided for since pupils differ in science achievement.

Teaching English Language Learners (ELL) in Science

The science teacher needs to ascertain the present level of achievement of each learner in English as well as in the science unit being taught. This is necessary for the pupil to progress from the known to the unknown. Being ready for the ensuing is salient. Thus the science teacher must plan learning opportunities based on what the ELL knows and what is left to learn. Once this has been ascertained, he/she needs to implement resulting plans. For example, the science teacher may develop an experiment, in a science unit of study involving "evaporation", which all can see clearly in order to benefit from instructional procedures. Depending upon where these learners are in achievement, the teacher may point to the aquarium and pronounce its related abstract word "aquarium". Pupils here may also say the same word to reinforce what is being learned. This word may be posted in the classroom word wall. Thus, to show what happens to the water in the aquarium, the science teacher needs to mark the present water level. Pupils are encouraged to view the level of the water periodically. Understandable words are used to explain what to observe. Meaningful communication must take place. ELL pupils will, of course, notice that the water in the aquarium is going below the mark. This may be discussed in clear terminology. Why did the water go below the marked level? The writer observed the following given answers:

- the fish drank the water
- the aquarium leaks
- water was taken from the aquarium (Kehr, 2009).

Each of these hypotheses is discussed, such as taking a paper towel to show no leakage occurred. However, for the hypothesis of "fish drinking the water", the teacher may then use a glass quart jar, filled to the top with water. The water level is marked. ELL pupils may then notice, "There are no fish to drink the water." Periodically, pupils also observe that no water is taken from the jar at any time. They will observe the water level going below the marked level. If pupils fail to come up with an hypothesis, the teacher needs to write the word "evaporation" on the word wall, followed by a clear, concise explanation. At this point, ELL need to visit the school's playground on a particular day to notice a water puddle, followed by the water having evaporated the next day. It may not always be possible to notice all variables in one experiment. These experiments can bring to the ELL attention, of the water cycle. A published illustration or one dawn by the teacher might well be utilized for the explanation and discussion. Securing the interests and active involvement of ELL are paramount. They are greatly needed to optimize learning. All learning must be made as concretely as possible with objects and items used in experiments together with clarity in related discussions (National Research Council, 1996).

Sequentially, pupils may clearly observe a related experiment, whereby one variable also is tested, pertaining to two potted plants from the same/similar stock. The word "plant(s)" is shown on the word wall with an accompanying illustration. Pupils, too, notice that :

- the same soil is used in planting for both pots. The words "soil" and "pots" are pointed to when being identified on the word wall
- the same recommended amount of fertilizer is used for both
- the same amount of water, observed by pupils, is added to each pot
- the same amount of sunlight for each setting on the window sill (Ediger 2007).

Now, pupils hypothesize what will happen if one of the two plants is covered with a paper sack. They can observe each plant carefully and not jump to hasty conclusions. Writing up each experiment is salient, indicating what happened through observation and relating it to the original hypothesis

The next experiment may stress that one potted plant receives adequate water, while the other receives no water. Pupils then hypothesize and observe what is happening. For ELL, an experience chart may be written to summarize what happened in these experiments. Pupils present the content orally while the teacher records the content. Learners may see their own ideas recorded on the white wall. They are read aloud together with teacher guidance as he/she points to each word in the read aloud. Here, pupils are expanding their sight word vocabulary in reading meaningful content pertaining to the science experiment. An authentic, clearly visible, experiment with related words read aloud pertaining to the hypothesis is noticed as talk written down. The experience chart may be reread, as often as desired, thus aiding ELL in recognizing words in print. Reading aloud without teacher assistance is recommended once pupils develop feelings of security in reading the contents of the science experiment. This helps pupils in understanding the methods of science in conducting experiments as well as in reading subject matter.

During story hour, the teacher might read, orally, selected library books in science on the understanding level of ELL. The library books, in this situation, should relate to the science unit being taught. The first unit discussed above dealt with the concept of "evaporation," whereas the second dealt with plant needs including water. By reading aloud during story hour those library books which relate to the science experiments, pupils are expanding their knowledge and skills of relevant content. Vital questions may be raised by the teacher to stimulate learning and provide opportunities for oral communication skills. Relating subject matter helps ELL to retain ideas longer as compared to isolated content (Ediger, 2008).

The examples provided'above assist ELL to perceive relationships in reading activities as well as in experimentation. Additional science activities for ELL are the following :

- reading developmentally appropriate library books to expand leanings in ongoing lessons and units of study. These may also be read within a small committee whereby pupils help each other as needed in word recognition and meaning. The teacher monitors and assists as needed.

- reading subject matter from the adopted basal science textbook. The teacher reads aloud the first time while ELL follow along in their textbook. Pupils, when ready, may read aloud together the same selection. Questions and their respective answers need elaboration to check for understanding and to provide learners opportunities to practice using the English language. Scaffolding may be provided by the teacher whereby the learner may understand more complex ideas.
- viewing and listening to discussions on video-tape pertaining to content in an ongoing lesson/unit of study. The ELL need many opportunities to practice the use of English in different functional learning experiences.
- science words posted on the word wall may be reviewed and used in sentences. The teacher may model proper sentence structure as is necessary.
- journal writing needs to be stressed which is on the achievement level of ELL. The dated entries may be constructed by the group, typed by the teacher in a word processor and viewed on a large screen, and then copied in their respective journals. As growth in writing continues, ELL might well become increasingly independent in writing as sequential learnings progress.
- hands on approaches are useful since this emphasizes concrete learning situations while abstract ideas are read and discussed relating directly to what is being constructed.

IN CONCLUSION

There are selected principles of learning which need to be stressed when teaching ELL. The following are strongly recommended :

- objectives must be developmentally appropriate for the level of English and science content possessed.
- sequence in learning needs to be approached from the child's present achievement level. The science teacher should carefully observe when the sequence is too complex or too easy.
- subject-matter in science must be understood with meaning attached. The quality of ELL response to questions raised becomes a gauge to instruction.
- interest, developed and maintained in ongoing lessons and units of study is a prime motivator of learning.
- purpose in learning needs to be established for each science objective to be attained. Thus, learning is not for the sake of doing so but relevant reasons are involved.

Concrete materials must be used in teaching and learning situations as is utilized in experimentation. The materials used here can be observed with the English language attached to each during instruction which makes it possible for ELL to achieve and progress. Success in learning is salient. In addition to, or in place of non-available concrete materials, pictures and illustrations help ELL to make sense of the English

REFERENCES

Ediger, Marlow (2007), *School Science Education*. New Delhi, India: Discovery Publishing House.

Ediger, Marlow (2008), "Leadership in the School Setting," *Education*, 129 (1), 17-20.

Kehr, Linda (2009), "Designing Payloads," *Science and Children*,46 (9), 22-26.

National Research Council (1996), *National Science Education Standards*. Washington, DC: National Academy Press.

7

Methods of Teaching Science

There are a plethora of methods to use in teaching science. The science teacher needs to study and assess diverse approaches in teaching and learning situations. Innovative procedures may be tried out, and if found suitable, integrated into the science curriculum. Individual differences among students in the classroom need adequate provision. The needs of each student must be met. This requires the teacher to use diverse methods of teaching since students differ from each other in style(s) of learning, in science knowledge, and in intelligence(s) possessed (Ediger 2007).

The Student and the Teaching of Science

Technology use in schools continues to increase at a rapid rate. Computer Assisted Instruction (CAI) and its implementation has made teaching students as interacting with a programme in a computer. The science program used must relate directly to the unit of study being taught as well as being on the developmental level of the learner. Additional considerations include :

- evaluating the present status of the learner's achievement with a pre-test
- providing science subject-matter in a meaningful manner
- presenting drill and practice activities to fix knowledge in the mind of the learner
- assisting pupil interest in learning with a gaming approach
- assessing pupil knowledge by using a post-test
- walking learners through a sequence of soft ware teaching packages
- keeping a record of test scores to notice achievement (Wiske, 2004).

The level of subject-matter difficulty in science needs to be appropriate for student acquisition in CAI programmes. Science vocabulary terms used in each programme must assist students to attach meaning to ongoing experiences. Accuracy of subject-matter is inherent and does not contain offensive stereotype materials offensive to anyone. The purpose for interacting with CAI materials should be clear to the student. Quality sequence in learnings is important so that successful achievers are in evidence. Graphics, colour, and sound, should promote the learning of science. Each programme should assist students to learn, grow, and develop. Feedback to learners' responses provides necessary and valuable information for the ensuing items to be learned (Djeassilane, 2008).

Virtual reality is stressed in computerized instruction. Thus, experimentation, being at the heart of the science curriculum, is shown as meaningfully as possible. The following then becomes a part of virtual reality in using computer aided instruction :

- showing which objects such as wood, glass, or metals, are/are not attracted by magnets
- showing that air has weight and takes up space
- showing the affects of gravity using toy cars and an inclined plane

- showing the use of simple machines in performing work
- showing how work is calculated in using foot pounds.

Processes, also, may readily be shown on the monitor portraying complete metamorphoses of an insect such as an egg, larva, pupa, and adult, as in a butterfly (Zahra, 2008).

The CAI might well be compared with a more traditional, but recommended approach in teaching science. In an ongoing science unit, the teacher may show or involve pupils in doing an experiment, for example, on what plants need in order to grow. Two potted plants of similar stock may be shown to learners. The same amount of recommended fertilizer, water, and sunlight, among other necessary factors need to be kept constant initially. One variable needs to be tested in terms of plant needs such as placing a box over one of the two plants to observe what happens. In a period of time, pupils might well notice the affects of a plant not receiving sunlight. After the plant recovers, the next variable to control is omission of water for one of the two plants. This may be followed with testing additional variables in terms of what a plant needs to grow well. For each experiment, pupils :

- must possess adequate background information in order to understand each concept in the experiment
- need to perceive the purpose of each experiment
- should be actively involved in achieving
- must attach meaning to ongoing experiences (Ediger, 2008).

Inquiry learning works well with quality ongoing experiments. Curious pupils may hypothesize as to what will transpire in the experiment. They may then check the outcomes of their hypotheses through careful observation of the experiment. Good discussions, using proper criteria, will assist in involving all students in the activity. Critical and creative thinking as well as problem solving encourage pupils to engage in higher cognitive levels of thinking. Indepth learning might well then be in evidence. Additional extended learnings include reading about related concepts from the internet, the basal textbook, and/or science encyclopedias. Pupils may also :

- write up a science experiment
- participate in small group discussions
- do a related project, based upon science subject-matter being studied
- develop and present an oral report on a selected facet of the ongoing science unit
- make a model individually or within a committee setting (National Research Centre, 1996).

A variety of learning activities need to be provided to assist each pupil to select an activity to complete. The activity is challenging and yet achievable. *Scaffolding* is a valuable concept for the teacher to use in teaching and learning situations. Thus, if a pupil does not understand a generalization in science, the teacher may use a series of small steps sequentially in teaching to help the pupil achieve the original complex idea. Pupils, also, need to develop a monitoring approach of their ongoing learnings to notice if meaning is being attached. If meaning is lacking, the pupil must be aided to ask questions so that the unknown becomes knowable subject matter (Cuniff and McMillen, 1996).

Metacognition emphasizes that pupils "think about thinking". Thus in a problem-solving aqtivity in science, the pupil needs to think about the sequential steps used in coming up with a tentative solution. The learner then reflects upon involved processes used. Then too, in learning about vocabulary terms in an ongoing science unit of study, the pupil thinks about how these were learned and reflects upon the meanings attached. It is necessary to do this so that learnings are retained and used. In supervising university student teachers in the public schools, the cooperating teacher modeled the concept of metacognition aloud for pupils with the following vocabulary terms studied in context a few days/ weeks previously :

- properties of matter
- position and motion of objects
- light, heat, and magnetism.

The above-named physical science terms were then reviewed and rehearsed by pupils as an advantage in seeing a model of the application of metacognition. Learners need to use what has been achieved or it will become hazy or forgotten.

IN CLOSING

Two methods were discussed in teaching science. The CAI is highly structured which follows a programmed learning model. The pupil here interacts with a computer and software. Relevant learnings may be obtained with an interesting program, carefully sequenced.

The second method discussed emphasized a multi-media approach with pupil/teacher interaction. A variety of media were used in teaching and learning situations. Teachers need to become highly knowledgeable of each procedure and stress what meets individual needs of pupils in science (Horesji, 2003).

REFERENCES

Cuniff, Patricia A., and Janet K. McMillen (1996), "Field Studies," *The Science Teacher,* 63 (51) 55-60.

Djeassilane, N. (2008), Computer Aided Instruction (CAI) in Enhancing the Academic Achievement of Higher Secondary Students in Commerce. Ph D. thesis evaluated by the writer for a Alagappa University, Karaikudi- 630 003, India.

Ediger, Marlow (2007), *Science Curriculum and Instruction.* New Delhi, India: Discovery Publishing House.

Ediger, Marlow (2008), "Leadership in the School Setting," *Education,* 129 (1), 17-20.

Horesji, Martin (2003), "Making Technology Inclusive," *Science and Children,* 41 (3), 20-24.

National Research Center (1996), *National Science Education Standards.* Washington, DC: National Academy Press.

Wiske, S. (2004), "Use Technology to dig for Meaning," *Educational Leadership,* 63 (1).

Zahra, Anne (2008), "Limitless Images: Digital Photography in the classroom," *The Delta Kappa Gamma Bulletin,* 75 (1), 7-9, 17.

8

Teaching of Science

There are selected guidelines which are recommended in teaching science. These guidelines assist teachers in promoting learner achievement. First, pupils need to be engaged in ongoing lessons and units of study. This empathizes securing pupil interests. If pupils are not engaged, the chances are that more optimal achievement is not possible. A stimulating environment which captures learner attention is a must. Thus, in performing a science experiment, all pupils involved need to see the experiment clearly. They need to hypothesize as to its outcomes. The writer when supervising university student teachers in the public schools has noticed rather consistently how pupils' attention is drawn to a carefully planned experiment in science with recored learner hypotheses. There is much excitement as to what will transpire. Pupils pay careful attention to the experiment as it actually occurs. Equally exciting is for pupils to keep in mind during experimentation how each hypothesis relates to the ongoing experiment. Objective evidence is wanted to confirm or refute any hypothesis. Jumping to hasty conclusions must be avoided by learners and the teacher.

Second, meaning must be attached by learners to each concept and generalization being stressed. Failure to make sense of new learnings makes for difficulty to add understand content in ensuing lessons being emphasized. For each new concept in ongoing lessons, pupils need indepth learning from a variety of reference sources used to secure knowledge and skills. Indepth learnings assists pupils to build on these ideas for sequential subject matter emphasized.

Third, pupils should experience purpose in learning. With accepted purpose, pupils feel there are reasons for achieving and developing. Relevance in subject matter acquired in science stresses that vital facts, meanings, as well as main ideas can be used in school and in society. In reading science content from a basal textbook to check conclusions drawn from an experiment, pupils need to perceive purpose or reasons for these learnings. The teacher may state the purpose deductively or pupils may be asked questions to arrive at the reasons for reading inductively. Pupils may need assistance in the following when reading science subject matter :

- using context clues to identify unknown words
- establishing purposes for reading such as reading to secure a main idea or for reading critically and creatively
- summarizing information gleaned
- securing information related to a science experiment
- obtaining background information to do a project or to engage in problem solving.

Fourth, pupils achieve at different levels in science and provision must be made for each to achieve as optimally as possible. Diverse teaching materials related to vital science objectives of instruction need to be in the offing. Concrete, semi-concrete, as well as abstract materials of instruction used judiciously by the teacher should assist pupils to do well in science lessons and units of study. Learnings need to be adapted to the present achievement level of learners with quality ordered activities following. Generally, pupils need to learn inductively through inquiry methods. A multi-cultural environment for learning needs emphasis whereby pupils learn in an . atmosphere of respect and acceptance.

Fifth, learning styles of individual pupils must be respected. Thus, selected pupils learn best in a cooperative learning setting whereas others do better on individual projects and activities. However, it is good for all to learn to work together harmoniously since schooling involves a social situation and pupils also must learn to work together in society. At the same time, pupils individually need to be responsible for finding worthwhile tasks during spare time in school and in society.

9

Readiness for Learning in Science

Readiness is an important factor in learning. This is true of any lesson and unit of study in science. The science teacher must make decisions pertaining to prerequisites which have/have not been mastered prior to stressing pupils achieving a new objective. If pupils are not ready for the ensuing learnings, they might experience frustration. New objectives must be challenging and yet be achieveable by the learner. Enjoyment and excitement in learning are salient in science to make for more optimal progress.

The science teacher must be well-prepared for each day of teaching so that pupils might attain relevant objectives, experience stimulating learning activities, as well as quality evaluation techniques which provide feedback to the teacher as well as pupils to improve the curriculum (Ediger, 2007).

Readiness and the Learner

How is readiness secured within pupils? One salient factor is to have learners possess adequate background information in order to benefit from ensuing experiences. Thus, in order to benefit from a unit on magnetism and electricity, pupils need selected understandings. The teacher, depending upon the maturation level of involved pupils, may have different materials in paper cups such as bits of paper, wood, steel nails, marbles, and cereal. Pupils individually might then hypothesize which items from the separate cups will be attracted by a bar or horse shoe magnet. Responses need to be recorded.

Additional readiness may be emphasized such as testing a suspended bar magnet from string with another magnet to determine if like poles attract or repel. Most pupils enjoy these activities. They also like to experiment with magnets on their own. These experiences, among others, provide readiness for pupils to benefit more fully from the new unit on magnetism and electricity. With needed prerequisite learnings, pupils are better able to achieve challenging objectives of instruction. The readiness experiences need to harmonize sequentially with the new learnings to be acquired. A seamless science curriculum is an end result (Gilbert and Kotelman, 2005).

In addition to having met readiness prerequisites, pupils also must perceive purpose in and for an ensuing unit of study. Purpose for learning resides within the pupil, not within the teacher. The latter assists in setting the stage for pupils perceiving purpose or reasons for learning. Reasons for attaining objectives then are in evidence. To perceive purpose, the pupil needs to become engaged in ongoing learning activities and intrinsically accept reasons for active participation. The teacher may briefly explain a purpose for the ensuing lesson, foe example, by stating why pupils need to experience a unit on electricity and magnetism. This may be done, for example, by indicating through AV aids how useful magnets are by picking up heavy loads of metal to be loaded onto a truck. The principle here of opposite poles attract is being emphasized such as a north pole attracting a south pole. If a teacher stated purpose does not motivate, then having pupils hypothesize reasons for learning about magnets might well be stressed. Generally, pupils come up with one or more reasons (National Research Council, 1996).

Third, pupils must experience interest in learning as a readiness factor. Interest propels pupil achieving of objectives of instruction. The learning opportunity and the learner become one and not separated from each other. If separation of the two occur, then perhaps little learning takes place. Hopefully, the pupil will become interested to the point that wholehearted involvement is in evidence. Due to interest, there are times when a pupil may desire to have the time extended for learning and achievement in science. Interest is a vital criterion to stress in science learning. When supervising university student teachers in the public schools, the writer noticed primary grade pupils huddled around an aquarium discussing the observed fish swimming. They discussed and raised many questions such as how gills operate for fish to survive underwater. The natural environment provides a plethora of interest centers for pupils. Outside of the school setting, pupils notice interesting phenomenon such as why a mud puddle dried up, after a rain. Here, the pupil may learn about the water cycle such as moisture in the form of rain followed by needed factors for evaporation. Also, pupils may bring science objects to school for show and tell experiences which, for example, might well include tadpoles in a jar from a farm pond. These tadpoles will then be observed to notice the growth of feet and eventually become a mature frog. Excitement is in the air with pupil eagerness to tell about their show and tell objects (Blough and Schwartz 1984).

Fourth, a quality current events program in science might well provide readiness for learning. In any newscast or news paper for children, there are a plethora of incidences which have just occurred. Thus, news items such as the following have occurred in different areas of the world;

- earthquakes, tornados, hurricanes

- mudslides, volcanic eruptions, gully and sheet erosion
- ice storms, floods, drought, hail, and strong wind gusts

Each of the above provide content for elaboration and discussions. Audio visual aids provide for clarity in current events presentations. Problem-solving activities may occur through identifying a problem pertaining to the causes of each of the above, developing an hypothesis, evaluating the hypothesis, and making necessary modifications and revisions. Indepth learnings may then occur.

At the beginning of the primary school years, pupils already may develop conclusions in problem-solving based on their individual maturity levels. All science teaching includes the following considerations :

- are the learnings on the understanding level of individual pupils?
- might pupils be motivated to realize high expectations?
- will the content be sequenced appropriately for optimal pupil progress?
- may indepth learning follow the readiness experiences? (Maheshwari, 2008).

Fifth, pupils need assistance to scaffold information. If, for example, a pupil did not attach meaning to the concept "reptiles", the science teacher may scaffold sequential activities to aid in its understanding. Depending upon the maturity level of the learner, the teacher might show pictures in the basal science textbook of snakes and turtles and briefly/clearly state why these are reptiles. The learner may verbalize, in return, what a reptile is to provide feedback to the teacher in revealing its understanding. With scaffolding, the pupil is able to learn more complicated subject matter than otherwise would be the case. Subject-matter chosen for scaffolding must be achievable, not beyond the capability of the pupil. The science teacher needs to receive feedback from the learner to notice if efforts at scaffolding have worked. If not, additional strategies need to be in the offing (Vygotsky, 1933, 1978).

Sixth, metacognition must be stressed. Here, the pupil reflects upon what has/has not been learned. Thus, a pupil thinks about previous learnings to notice if readiness exists to acquire the ensuing subject matter. The science teacher, also, must reflect upon previously used teaching strategies to notice what worked and what did not work effectively. Modifications in teaching might then be made such as in the following :

- from the use of abstract learnings to emphasizing concrete experiences for pupils
- from rote learning to problem solving activities
- from lecture to inquiry learning
- from reading about science to doing science as in performing experiments, the heart of the science curriculum
- from being passive recipients of knowledge to actively pursuing tasks as in the project method
- from memorizing science subject matter to engaging in problem solving.

Seventh, learning styles (Searson and Dunn, 2001) have salient implications for teaching and learning. To provide readiness for learning, each pupil prefers a particular style more so than others. Thus, selected pupils may prefer cooperative learning rather than experiencing individual activities. The former have preferences to learn within a committee setting as compared to the latter who prefer to engage in learning opportunities by the self. For example in using the project method, a set of learners select to work together in developing a model volcano in an ongoing unit of study, whereas another pupil chooses to work on a model pertaining to folding and faulting individually. Further differences in styles of learning include the following :

- teacher guided instruction as compared to an open ended science curriculum
- a subject centred science curriculum instead of using pupil centered procedures
- the use of behaviourally stated objectives in instruction versus open ended objectives in teaching and learning situations
- a separate subject science curriculum versus integrated units of study relating many academic disciplines.

The science teacher then must take into consideration under which conditions pupils learn best in ongoing lessons and units of study. Optimal pupil achievement is desired and therefore learning styles need consideration in choosing activities and experiences. Readiness for learning requires that science teachers take into consideration how pupils learn.

Eighth, readiness for learning must also take into consideration multiple intelligences theory. Thus, a pupil may possess one or more intelligences in the acquisition of knowledge and skills. Science has its own methods and subject-matter. However, related content from other disciplines might assist pupils to achieve more optimally. The following intelligences may be brought in as needed to clarify and extend subject-matter learnings :

- verbal as in reading and writing experiences
- logical as in reasoning about science phenomenon
- musical as in writing lyrics directly related to science and putting the words to music
- intrapersonal as in showing much strength in working by the self

- interpersonal as in revealing considerable achievement in cooperative learning
- bodily/kinesthetic as in doing high quality projects and construction work
- scientific intelligence in thinking objectively in learnings dealing with the natural and social environment (Gardner, 1993).

Ninth, portfolios might well assist the science teacher in determining pupil readiness for learning. Traditional or digital portfolios contain a representative sampling of pupil work in science lessons and units of study such as the following :

- book reports on science content
- photos of science projects and construction work, individually and/or committee endeavors
- sample recordings of oral reading and communication activities
- results from teacher written and standardized tests
- self evaluation in terms of recommended criteria
- art work products completed in science lessons and units of study
- creative written work as in writing poems and stories:

By examining each of the above in terms of pupil present achievement, the science teacher is better able to ascertain pupil readiness for learning as well as to assess pupil progress (Ediger, 2008-2009).

Tenth, a variety of evaluation procedures need to be used to ascertain learner achievement in science. These procedures must be valid and reliable, using the best criteria in the evaluation process when using:

- teacher written tests
- standardized and mandated tests
- teacher observation
- product and process evaluation.

REFERENCES

Blough, Glenn O., and Julius Schwartz (1984), *Elementary School Science and How To Teach It.* New York: Holt, Rinehart and Winston.

Ediger, Marlow (2007), *School Science Education.* New Delhi, India: Discovery Publishing House.

Ediger, Marlow (2008-2009) "Portfolios in Science," *Connecticut Journal of Science Education,* 47 (1), 28-29.

Gilbert, Jean, and Marleen Kotelman (2005), Five Good Reasons to use Science Notebooks," *Science and Children,* 43 (3), 28-32.

Gardner, Howard (1993), *Multiple Intelligences: Theory Into Practice.* New York: Basic Books.

Maheshwari, Amrita (2008), "Integral Values of Science Education," *Edutracks,* 8 (4), 16-17.

National Research Council (1996), *National Science Education Standards.* Washington, DC: National Academy Press.

Searson, Robert and Rita Dunn (2001), "The Learning Styles Teaching Model," *Science and Children,* 38 (5), 22-36.

Vygotsky, L. S. (1933, 1978), *Mind in Society: The Development of Higher Psychological Processes.* Cambridge, Massachusetts: Harvard University Press.

10

Parent/Teacher Conferences and Science Curriculum

In an increasingly complex society, all pupils need to possess high levels of literacy in science. The news media is filled with items pertaining to the natural world such ad hurricanes, tornados, earthquakes, tsunamis, drought, floods, and mudslides, among others. Science has provided the lay public with modern technology to make life easier and more convenient. Modern appliances, cooling and heating systems, means of transportation, and processes in food preservation, among others, have used principles of science to improve society. The world of science needs to be used to improve society and the human condition. It can also be used for destructive purposes. Knowledgeable persons need to make rational decisions based on the solving of problems in terms of which direction science and technology may move forward (Ediger, 2007).

Parents need to be well informed of their offspring's progress in science learnings. Parent/teacher conferences might well assist parents to understand pupil achievement more fully. These conferences need to follow selected criteria. There needs to be respect among participants in order for quality communication to occur. Rudeness and intimidation have no roles to play in a conference. Participants need to feel free to ask questions and make comments pertaining to the child's progress in science. Each must seek to learn as much as possible about how well the learner is achieving in ongoing science lessons and units of study (National Science Teachers Association, 2001).

The science teacher needs to be well-prepared for the conference and parents, too, need to identify questions and problems involving the offspring's progress. This provides a setting for a profitable conference.

What should the science teacher have available for the parent/teacher conference to show parents in terms of learner products? If a portfolio has been kept, this would make for a device to show progress in science achievement. Among others, the science portfolio will usually contain the following representations of a pupil's work :

- written book reports of science library books read
- digital pictures of science experiments and committee work engaged in
- summaries of science experiments and demonstrations
- sample pages from science journals and diaries kept.

From the above items, parents may ask questions of the science teacher such as the following :

- Is the pupil making adequate progress overall in science?
- What can we do at home to assist the child to improve in achievement?
- Might selected science experiments be done at home with the child?
- How can the learner be assisted in reading and writing in science?
- How may the use of computers assist pupil progress (Ediger 1990)?

Each of the above needs to be discussed in depth with the intent of assisting the child to improve in science knowledge, skills, and attitudes. There needs to be an agreement of what the home and school will do to help the pupil achieve more optimally. The science teacher needs to secure relevant information from parents to assist the child in future science learnings. Information such as the following is vital for the science teacher to guide pupil progress :

- does the child ask interesting questions involving science? Science is everywhere and the child needs to be aware of this. Pupils have asked why the water level goes down in the living room aquarium containing gold fish, or what happens when a mud puddle becomes dry in summer time.
- do you visit science museums, if available, in your area? The point is to visit interesting places with the child where science learnings are stimulated. Most cities have museums where science learning is stressed. A traveling display of dinosaurs in a small university museum captured the interests of many students. Seeing the skeletal remains of the brontosaurs, the dipladocus, the stegosaurs, among others, is fascinating to all. Parents should learn together with their children. Supon (2006) wrote the following pertaining to the use of digital cameras to film important phenomenon.

Digital camera use increases analytical skills and can be used as a means of assessing student performance. Having students know what high quality performance is can effectively be documented through photographs. When students recognize similarities and differences of their performance through photos, students become reflective and effective with self-assessment. This process increases performance.

- do you read science library books together and discuss their contents? A good collection of science books is important in the home setting. Library books may be checked out free from the school and city library.

Science literacy is for all. Pertaining to science literacy, Zales and Unger (2008) wrote the following :

> Reading captivating stories - both fiction and non-fiction- provide enjoyment for students, through both the text and the illustrations. Carefully selected trade books can introduce science concepts, develop background knowledge, reinforce hands-on lessons, support process skills and at the same time enhance science literacy process skills. They can also provide inspiration and structure for integrated science and literacy lessons.

Parent teacher conferences may be carried out by using a variety of approaches. Face to face interaction, in a caring manner, is, probably, the best procedure. However, there are additional procedures such as telephone calls, e-mail, and letter writing.

IN CONCLUSION

There are key concepts to emphasize in the science curriculum. The following are salient :

- *problem solving*. This involves critical and creative thinking to secure answers to questions involving dilemmas
- *objectivity*. Students are to think and observe as things really are, without personal biases and prejudices
- *inquiry learning*. Students need to learn by discovery methods
- *key structural content in science subject matter*. These are major generalizations, concepts, and facts, vital in academic science learning
- *use of science equipment*. Here, students need to make applicable the methods of science by using modern technology.

REFERENCES

Ediger, Marlow (2007), *School Science Education.* New Delhi, India: Discovery Publishing House.

Ediger, Marlow (1990), *Role of Philosophy in Teaching Science,"* Paideia, Published by the Polish Academy of Science, Warsaw, Poland, pp. 242-246.

National Science Teachers Association (2001), Classroom Assessments and the National Education Standards. Washington DC: NSTA.

Supon, Viola (2006), "Using Digital Cameras for Multidimensional Learning," *Journal of Instructional Psychology*, 33 (1), 154-156.

Zales, Charlotte Rappe, and Connie S. Unger (2008), "The Science and Literacy Framework," *Science and Children*, 46 (3), 42-45.

11

Poetry in Science Curriculum

There are a plethora of purposes in writing in the science curriculum. Writing serves a variety of reasons. One purpose is to *use* acquired knowledge. Poetry writing is one approach for the learner to apply what has been learned in ongoing science units of study. Poetry writing has a fascination of its very own. Learners seemingly enjoy writing verse containing rhyme as well as the unrhymed. For each type of poem written, students need to possess readiness factors which include :

- knowledge of characteristics of each kind of poem to be written
- adequate fluency in writing diverse kinds of poetry
- functional abilities in spelling
- positive attitudes toward poetry
- reading poetry with meaning (Ediger, 2008).

The science teacher then needs to ascertain if students are ready to write poetry in its many forms.

Motivation to Write Poetry

The writer supervised university student teachers for thirty years in the public schools and observed many student teachers and cooperating teachers motivate pupils in diverse kinds of writing activities (Mesa *et al.*, 2008).

Student motivation is salient in studying and writing of poems. Developmentally appropriate activities need to be in the offing.The science teacher needs to model reading aloud each kind of poem which will be written in sequence. The first kind of poem may be the couplet. Thus, after a science couplet has been read, the teacher may print it for all students to see. A discussion should follow whereby students inductively discover the two lines of verse with ending words rhyming. Generally, the two lines are somewhat equivalent in length. The science teacher may then assist pupils to recall what was studied in the ongoing science unit of study. Acquired facts, concepts, and generalizations might well become a significant part of a couplet (See National Research Council, 1996). It is important for the teacher to share a science couplet he/she wrote. The following is an example :

Winter

Cold weather and snow
Help the cold wind blow.

Pupils tend to like experimenting with what has been learned in science in writing couplets. Most like to share orally their individual written couplet with classmates. In this way, pupils review what has been learned and apply these learnings to a new situation. Many student teachers and regular teachers in the public schools, supervised by the writer, had an anthology of children's literature on their desk tops containing interesting poems, related to the present unit being studied.

In sequence, triplets may be studied which contain three lines of rhyme with the lines somewhat uniform in length. Pupils in small groups may desire to write a triplet collectively

(Ediger, 2002). A committee of pupils in a public school wrote the following triplet:

Hail

The spring weather was quite pleasant
Followed by a cooling down of each plant
With pieces of ice from the sky falling at a slant.

Quatrains generally contain four lines of verse with lines one and two as well as lines three and four rhyming or all four lines may rhyme. When pupils posses the needed prerequisites, the science teacher may provide motivational background experiences to stimulate quatrain writing (Ediger, 2007). A quatrain written by a fifth grade pupil contained the following subject matter:

Erosion

With no cover crop for the moisture to hold
A very heavy rain caused soil to erode
Trees and grass may have slowed the runoff bold
Wasted top soil hinders production of future crops to be sold .

Pupils should be asked to share, orally, their poems. Each poem read aloud needs to be received by classmates in an atmosphere of respect. Poems might then be posted on a poetry wall for all to read in the classroom. Learning from each other is important (Pardo, 2004)!

A very interesting kind of poem to write is the limerick. Teacher's anthologies of children's literature contain limericks which should be read aloud in the classroom. Any poem read aloud needs to be read with enthusiasm. Voice inflection with proper stress and pitch of each word needs to be emphasized. The science teacher's voice may be used effectively to secure learner attention. Once pupils have carefully noticed that a limerick contains rhyme in lines one, two, and five, as well as lines three and four rhyming, they need encouragement to apply what has been learned (Cochran-Smith, 2006). A cooperating teacher wrote and read orally the following model for student contemplation :

Thomas Edison
There once was a great inventor
Who gave the world much light as a vendor
He worked hard until it was perfected
With the incandescent light bulb as he intended
Edison lives forever as our mentor.

Syllabication and Poetry in Science

Selected pupils like to write verse containing a pattern of syllabication, with no expected rhyme. Haiku is a kind of poem built upon five, seven, five syllables for each sequential three lines of poetry. Pupils need to listen to and see several haiku before actually writing a haiku as an ensuing writing experience. A sixth grader wrote the following :

Rocks and minerals
Beautiful, useful, handy
Buildings, and fine gems.

The haiku may be extended by adding two lines with seven and seven syllables for each of two lines, making for a tanka. Or, learners may prefer to write a completely new tanka on a different topic studied in science. A student teacher wrote the following which was read aloud to pupils and served as a model for writing :

Tornados, lonely, dark
funnels in the blue rimmed sky
descending from high
very strong winds rushing by
with cone shaped skyward motion.

Selected pupils, when ready, may wish to write free verse, containing no rhyme nor syllables per line. There are a plethora of forms used in writing free verse. The following model was developed and read to students by a cooperating teacher:

Reptiles consist of turtles, crocodiles, alligators, and snakes

are cold blooded and sluggish in cold weather
move slowly in the environment
live in water and on land
generally have lungs
eat plants and animals.

The final poem, a diamante, which is diamond shaped should be developed cooperatively by students with teacher guidance.

Soil	(consisting of a single noun)
heavy, moist	(two adjectives)
planting, growing, weeding	(three participles)
Clay, loam, igneous, sedimentary	(four nouns)
plowing, disking, harrowing	(three participles)
dusty, murky	(two adjectives)
dirt	(noun).

IN CLOSING

Values inherent in the writing of poetry in science are numerous. It provides opportunities to put science vocabulary terms to use. Knowledge which is used is less likely to be forgotten. Playing around with science vocabulary assists pupils to be creative when engaged in writing poetry. Creativity is salient in school and in society. Unique, novel ways are needed to come up with innovations in society (Kennedy, 2008).

REFERENCES

Cochran-Smith, Marilyn (2006), "Ten Promising Trends (and Three Big Worries," *Educational Leadership*, 63 (6), 20-25.

Ediger, Marlow (2008), "Leadership in the School Setting," *Education*, 129.

Ediger, Marlow (2002), *Teaching Language Arts Successfully*. New Delhi, India: Discovery Publishing House.

Ediger, Marlow (2007), *School Science Education*. New Delhi, India: Discovery Publishing House.

Kennedy, Mary (2008), "Sorting Out Teaching Quality," *Phi Delta Kappan*, 90 (1), 59-63.

Mesa,Jennifer C. *et al.* (2008), The P.O.E.T.R.Y Of Science," *Science and Children*, 46 (3), 36-41.

National Research Council (1996), National Science Education Standards. Washington, DC: National Academy Press.

Pardo, Laura (2004), "What Every Teacher Needs to Know About Comprehension," *The Reading Teacher*, 58(3), 27.

12

Constructivism and Science Curriculum

Constructivism is a psychological term emphasized in the school curriculum. It stresses pupils, individually or collectively, to be central or at the heart in ongoing learning activities. Science objectives, learning activities, and evaluation techniques are pupil centred. This presents a unique paradigm and role for the science teacher. He/she no longer is the central actor in the classroom, but provides opportunities for pupils to be dominant members in ongoing lessons and units in the science curriculum. The pupil is the learner and must be encouraged to achieve, learn, and grow.

A Constructivist Teacher

Which beliefs and educational philosophies do constructivist teachers adhere to? They tend to emphasize student autonomy. Lecturing to students during class time in diverse academic areas fails to stress learner initiative. Rather, teacher/pupil planning of science objectives, learning experiences, and appraisal procedures involve engagement of pupils in making curricular decisions. Students are encouraged to be actively involved in determining their curriculum, rather than being passive recipients of knowledge and skills. Being able to accept students who are actively involved as decision makers in the curriculum may be difficult for some teachers, but for the constructivist teacher this is an ideal (Padmanabhan, 2007).

Thus, within a peer mediated discussion group, students accept full responsibility for decisions made during discussions. They may make decisions, for example, on a peer project which involves doing a mural/chart on Prehistoric Life including the Paleozoic Era, the Mesozoic Era, and the Cenozoic Era. Drawings of animal life during each era should be made neatly, clearly showing the major kinds which existed. For example, during the Mesozoic Era, the Age of Dinosaurs was very much in existence and should be shown on the mural. These drawings and their respective history are fascinating to many pupils. Selected dinosaurs were plant eaters, others were meat eaters, while still others may be classified as plant and animal eaters. The kinds of vegetation as it existed in the Mesozoic Era may be shown as background information. Careful planning and accurate drawings must be made (National Research Council (NRC), 1996).

With involvement of students in individual/committee endeavors, the constructivist teacher is able to secure learner interest in an ongoing science unit of study. Learner planning of the project brings to bear, criteria, which need to be incorporated to assess the completed project as well as of the processes involved. The planning of the project is open ended and provides numerous opportunities in decision making (Ediger and Rao, 2007).

A Learning Community

A model learning community formed on the local level will be discussed along with how it can assist in improving the curriculum. A learning community represents a powerful way of obtaining cooperation among diverse levels of participation such as students and faculty; school administrators and parents; the lay public; leaders from business and industry; as well as labor and union representatives. Each of these groups needs a chair person and a secretary. Which curriculum area needs emphasis for a given school year? Assuming that science receives priority for the ensuing school year. Science was omitted in statewide testing under the No Child Left Behind Law until the 2007-2008 school year. Thus, an innovative approach such as a learning community may well help in working closely together and raise student achievement levels in science. This is a major effort in planning, implementing, and assessing quality in the curriculum. Each group needs to choose an area of interest and develop that facet of science achievement harmoniously. Thus, a large group session may be held to ascertain the direction of its goals. Areas of interest from which community members might well choose may be the following :

- volunteering one's services in the regular classroom by reading loud to children during story time, listening to pupil read alouds and assisting in word recognition techniques, checking pupil papers and going over the errors with the involved pupil. This might also emphasize assisting pupils on the playground and in the lunchroom. Making room for the needs of children is salient.
- objectives for student achievement in the science curriculum. The set of objectives chosen for learners to achieve needs to represent the concept of excellence. Here, volunteers may survey different sets of objectives put out by the national Science Teachers Association, the Association for Supervision and Curriculum Development, and the National Association of Elementary School Principals, among other national organizations in education. Statewide affiliates of each may also bring to bear objectives of instruction written for pupil achievement. Each state

has a science teachers affiliate of the parent organization. Objectives gleaned and summarized and might then be compared with the local statement of science teaching objectives. A discussion of objectives in science teaching makes for a problem solving situation when the best are selected from among alternatives.

- providing for individual differences among learners. There are a plethora of differences among children in any classroom. Pupils individually need assistance in the learning activities provided. Word recognition problems in reading may well account for several volunteers to help pupils. Understanding subject matter read may cause problems to some unless aid is available. Higher levels of cognition raises the bar in comprehension of content. Inferential reading as well as critical and creative reading involve comprehension, but are at different levels of complexity. The science teacher may work with pupils in these skills while a volunteer is assisting a set of pupils in word recognition in independent reading of library books directly related to the unit being taught in science. The latter group also will have equivalent time for higher levels of thinking activities within a small group.
- the separate subjects versus the integrated science curriculum. This continues to be an issue. Holism in the curriculum stresses science subject matter be integrated with social studies, literature, and mathematics, where feasible. But integration of content should not be stressed for the sake of doing so, but rather that it serves a useful purpose. For example, in cases of natural disasters including earthquakes, tornados, and mud slides, pupils need to explain the causes of each scientifically and objectively. To remedy human suffering from these

natural disasters, social services are involved. The vast array of organizations and groups which provide these services need to be studied. Thus, science and the social studies become integrated entities.

- learning activities to achieve objectives. These need to be varied and provide for indepth learning. Concrete experiences are one category. These consist of using real objects in teaching and learning such as in conducting science experiments. This might well branch out to semi-concrete activities, such as seeing and discussing a power point presentation related directly to the science experiment. Each slide in the experience needs to expand indepth from the previous activity. The third category of learning experiences emphasizes the abstract phase of learning and includes reading to secure more information pertaining to the ongoing experiment, as welt as to write up its findings in approved form (Ediger, 2002).
- constructivism in the science curriculum. Here, committee members may study explicit, direct teaching of subject matter as compared to constructivism with considerable input into ongoing science units. For example, the science teacher may perform the science experiment as compared to pupils being more involved in, or completely doing the experiment with teacher guidance (Mansilla and Gardner, 2008).
- project methods in the science curriculum. This procedure may involve much of constructivism in science whereby pupils in a small group decide upon a project within the ongoing science unit of study. Thus, a purpose is established in a construction activity. The purpose may be to make models of a volcano, soil erosion, as well as folding and faulting. Careful plans must be in the offing to make each model. Accuracy, proper proportion, and realism is important. The plans made need to be carried out, with

modifications made as needed. The completed projects need evaluation in terms of definite criteria, such as in a rubric. The completed projects may be displayed for other classrooms to observe (Burton, 2005).

- assessment of student processes. Here, the students' participation skills need assessment such as all in the small group need to participate with no one dominating. Quality group dynamics are salient. Ideas from participants need to be respected. Ideas presented must circulate within the committee. Clarity of ideas must be meaningful to participants. Assessment must inform instruction. Thus, results from the assessment provide information for sequential instruction.

For each of the above named areas, seven to eight community members may volunteer/choose on which committee to serve. The first category, volunteering one's services in the classroom, a somewhat endless number might well serve in different capacities.These would center around helping the science teacher to provide for each pupil in the classroom. Each committee needs to report on their endeavors to keep other groups informed. Questions will arise on clarity of ideas presented and also on how specific strategies will be implemented.

There are specifics which need to be worked out pertaining to meetings for the small groups. These include the time and place of meeting dates. Input from participants should focus on the most appropriate time for all, realizing there will be conflicts. Should refreshments be served? It would be good to do so, but this decision needs to be left up to the participants.

Two Schools of Thought Pertaining to Constructivism

There are basically two schools of thought which stress constructivist philosophy of education. Jean Piaget, educated as a biologist, studied children for over 15 years in Geveva, Switzerland and wrote, in his research, about four stages which children go through to reach adulthood. From birth through two years of age, the child is in the sensori-motor stage of development. The child in this stage uses the five senses and motor skills in learning. From ages two to seven, the child is in the stage of preoperational development. The child focuses upon one variable such seeing the height or width, only, of an object. Biological maturation on an individual basis is involved in growing from one stage to the next and this cannot be hastened. The child basically selects what to learn and what to interact with in sequence. This is not based on group norms or standards.

The stage of concrete operations begins at age seven years of age and here the child learns from objects and items in the environment, as was done previously, but the use of the abstract such as reading, writing, listening, and speaking, are becoming increasingly stronger and supplement/clarify the real objects and situations observed. Highly meaningful learnings accrue when words (the abstract), illuminate the related items observed and studied.

Piaget's fourth stage is represented, in maturation, by the stage of formal thought. There is much less of a need, here, to focus upon the concrete. The pupil now may focus discussion and thought upon the abstract only. Adults tend to use the abstract only while interacting, and yet meaningful transcriptions occur.

Piaget's theory of maturation stresses individual stages of growth regardless of peers growth levels.

In comparison to Piaget, Vygotsky (1933/1978) came out with a social theory of constructivism. Here, pupils work together collectively in ensuing lesson(s) to realize facts, concepts, and generalizations. As pupils interact, their ideas modify and change. As thoughts circulate within the small group, they emphasize sequential progress. It is pupils then within a committee, who generate subject matter within a lesson or unit of study. The small group rather than the individual come up with content to realize objectives of instruction (Hoy and Miskel, 2006).

Reflective Teaching

With reflection, the science teacher reviews mentally what has just transpired in teaching and learning in the classroom. He/she now has opportunities to think about how well learners were engaged in the ensuing lesson. Were there pupil questions which might have been a springboard for indepth learning? Was each child enthused for learning? If not, what might have been emphasized to include all in actively engaged learning? Were the learning experiences appropriate when providing for individual differences? These, among other questions, require reflective thinking.

Pupils, too, need to reflect upon what was achieved during an ongoing science lesson. They need to reflect upon the following :

- Did I pay attention to the ongoing science experiment?
- What was not clear in the presentation?
- Which questions do I need to have answered?
- Which subject matter possessed clarity and meaning?

By reflecting upon what was taught, the learner is able to pinpoint vague facts, concepts, and generalizations. Then too, the pupil is able to focus upon faulty processes used in learning. These learnings might well improve sequence in pupil achieving. Thus, better order of content acquired might well increase overall achievement and progress in science (Savithiri, 2006).

The science teacher must stay abreast of current trends in teaching. This is true for professional reasons as well as fro assisting pupils to achieve. He/she may update knowledge an skills through the following means :

- taking graduate course work in science content and science education. The science teacher who has a good command of subject matter knowledge is better able to assist pupils in indepth learning about any topic being studied in an ongoing lesson or unit of study. Also, with an increase in knowledge and skill pertaining to science education, the teacher may assist the learner more proficiently where questions and problems arise within a specific learning activity. Today's pupils are more knowledgeable than learners previously. It behooves the science teacher to remain updated in teaching and learning strategies.
- read information on teaching science from reputable journals. A professional area in school for stocking materials on science instruction is a must for classroom teachers.
- taking courses online is a definite possibility for science teachers. They may then budget their time appropriately and keep possibilities open for engagement in learning when it is convenient to do so.
- doing an independent study on induction in science teaching is a further possibility. The independent study online or on campus from an accredited university must take into consideration depth and breadth. A quality science teacher should be an end result.
- observing good teachers teach science. Before and after the observational visit, the visiting teacher needs to have a detailed conference with the one exhibiting excellence in teaching (See also Horejsi, 2003).

The goal involved in each of the above named inservice education programmes is to strengthen science teaching. The science teacher is then better able to help pupils to achieve, grow, and learn. Instead of providing a direct answer to a problem, the science teacher is able to ask further questions leading the leaner to find his/her own answer. Constructivism emphasizes the use of learner input into the curriculum. In this way, pupils may assist in determining the science curriculum.

REFERENCES

Burton, Kimberly Smith (2005), "Using Student Peer Evaluations to Examine Team Taught Lessons," *Journal of Instructional Psychology*, 32 (2), 136-138.

Ediger, Marlow (2002), "The Supervisor of the School," *Education*, 122 (3), 602-604.

Ediger, Marlow, and D. Bhaskara Rao (2007), *School Science Education.* New Delhi, India: Discovery Publishing House.

Horejsi, Martin (2003), "Making Technology Inclusive," *Science and Children*, 41 (3), 20-24. Published by the National Science Teachers Association (NSTA).

Hoy, Wayne K., and Cecil G. Miskel (2006), *Educational Administration, Theory, Research, and Practice.* New York: Me Graw Hill, Inc.

Mansilla, Veronica Boix, and Howard Gardner (2008), "Disciplining the Mind," *Educational Leadership*, 65 (5), 14-19.

National Research Council (NRC). 1996.

National Science Education Standards (1996), Connecting to the Standards. Washington, DC: National Academy Press.

Padmanabhan, Vasundhara (2007), "Constructivism and Reflective Teaching in Teacher Education, *Edutracks*, 7 (4),14-16. Published in India.

Savithiri, V. (2006), Impact of Metacognitive Strategies in Enhancing Perceptual Skills Among High School Students on Learning Geometry. Ph D University, India.

13

Developing Student Interest in Science

Interest is a powerful factor in learning. It almost appears that interest in science is innate for young children. They seemingly are intrigued with the natural environment. Young children have abundant energy for asking many different kinds of questions. Kindergarten children, when walking, may come to school late due to seeing and observing such things as colorful butterflies on pleasant days. Much enthusiasm is shown for science phenomenon. Too frequently, as pupils grow older, they lose some curiosity. What might be done by the teacher to encourage continuous interest in science.

Metacognition in the Science Curriculum

Metacognition is an excellent concept to emphasize in teaching and learning situations. It stresses thinking about thinking. Thus, the pupil learns to monitor his/her own progress. When reading science subject matter, the learner evaluates if he/she is identifying words correctly. With metacognition, the pupil might well realize that improved methods of word recognition are possible. Perhaps, the reader realizes that context clues need to be used more frequently. The learner also must monitor if the content read is understood in what has, and is been read. Sometimes, a reader pronounces words but fails to attach meaning to the ensuing content. Word calling is then in evidence. Comprehension, however, is desired. By monitoring the reading activity, the pupil must notice if facts, concepts, and generalizations are understood. The pupil then is thinking about science content acquired during the reading experience. A lack of achievement may be noticed; more thorough concentration must then be emphasized. The science teacher needs to model to students how metacognition works in the curriculum. Thus, the teacher may read aloud a given passage and then state in his/her own words content which has been read. Small group work might well be necessary for pupils taking turns in silent/oral reading and then indicate orally subject matter read in the learner's own words. Each pupil would take his/her turn in reading a passage from the science basal/library book, and state what was comprehended. Learners must be aware of the necessity to comprehend well which is quite different then word calling. Being conscious of the need to comprehend carefully is highly important. Reading is done to comprehend ideas.

In performing science experiments, the pupil needs assistance to monitor sequence in problem solving. He/she then reflects upon how the problem was identified in the ongoing unit of study and then following through in assessing how the hypothesis was selected and tested. With metacognition, the pupil may think of better methods to use in doing science experiments. Retention of subject matter acquired and means used in problem solving might then be refined and improved upon (Ediger and Rao, 2007).

Self-efficacy and the Teacher

Being confident in one's own teaching stresses the concept of self-efficacy. The science teacher develop self efficacy by strengthening knowledge and skills used in teaching. He/

she needs to take graduate science coursework at accredited universities or colleges; A new avenue has opened up in taking classes online. This makes it possible for the teacher to complete courses at his/her convenience and doing this in the home setting. These are virtual courses and learning, taken online, may well bring in as much reality as possible.

Reading content from salient periodicals, teacher education textbooks, as well as attending professional meetings to acquire new ideas in teaching and learning should assist the teacher in developing feelings of self-confidence. Self-efficacy emphasizes the importance in believing one can be successful in teaching pupils from diverse ability levels, home backgrounds, as well as socio-economic levels. It is a powerful concept to stress when present achievement levels of pupils is based upon income levels of families and the socio-economic level of where the school is located. An attitude of competency in one's own teaching comes into the picture. With these positive feelings, self efficacy is being emphasized (Ediger, 2007).

Doing relevant science experiments which capture pupil interests is at the heart of ongoing lessons and units of study. Being able to write up the results of experiments is vital. The science teacher's competencies not only involve assisting pupils to engage in doing quality experiments, but also to be a teacher of reading science content as well as help learners in the area of written work. The write-up needs to include the problem, the hypothesis, the assessment of each hypothesis, as well as modifications made as a result of testing each. The written content should meet the following criteria, depending upon developmentally appropriate standards :

- proper sentence structure and correct spelling of words with proofing done in a collaborative setting
- clarity in ideas presented sequentially
- mechanics of writing stressed such as punctuation marks, capitalization of letters where necessary, and indentation of paragraphs.

- accuracy in writing about the experiment, including inherent subject matter.

Interest in writing should be shown with teacher enthusiasm reflected within pupils. Encouragement by the teacher, too, should assist positive pupil attitudes toward written work in science. Science teachers need to model quality written work for pupil observation. A relaxed environment must be in evidence so that pupils may think clearly when engaging in a variety of learning activities in the science curriculum as well as interest fostered in learning (Ediger, 2007b).

Scaffolding Pupil Learning in Science

Scaffolding may help pupils to develop interest in acquiring increasingly complex ideas. A scaffold assists in reaching higher when doing construction work or in painting different structures. In teaching, the science teacher must assist pupils to understand more complex ideas. A gap may exist between the pupil's present level of achievement in an ongoing lesson and an ideal to attain. Scaffolding as a concept may be used to fill the void. The science teacher or peers within a committee might well guide the pupil to achieve the ensuing objective, or ideal. This may be accomplished through :

- a discussion which explores ideas indepth
- viewing a power point or video tape
- reading from an assignment in a reference book to close the gap
- raising questions of the learner until he/she comes up with needed subject matter (Ediger, 2006).

Meaningful learnings acquired through scaffolding provide for challenge and interest. High expectations by the teacher for pupil progress in a developmentally appropriate science curriculum extends learner achievement in reaching toward higher, more complex objectives. This may be realized, also, through the use of learning centres. Centres of learning have been used by selected teachers for entire science units of study, replacing other approaches. The writer recommends setting up two or three centers in a classroom to encourage further learnings in science. The centres should be identified and briefly discussed with pupils in the classroom. Pupils may volunteer to complete work at the different centres to receive extra credit. A certain number of tasks, as a minimal number, at the two or three learning centres might also be required for each pupil to complete. Tasks selected would be open to pupil choice based on learner interest. When the science teacher writes the tasks (learning activities) for the different centres, securing student interest should be a prime consideration. Audio-visual aids, experimentation, reading and writing activities, a salient excursion to a nearby place, relevant to the ongoing science unit, might well provide necessary materials to use in gathering information for tasks chosen at at the diverse learning centres.

Interest is a powerful factor in securing pupil engagement in learning. Meaningful learnings encourage pupil interest in science. They must make sense to the learner. Thus, pupils understand what is being taught. Use of knowledge and skills acquired assist pupils to feel that science is salient in school and in society. This also increases pupil motivation for achieving objectives of instruction.

Many uses of knowledge in science can be made through higher levels of thinking. Noddings (2008) wrote the following pertaining to thinking :

> Writers often distinguish among thinking categories as critical thinking, reflective thinking, creative thinking, and higher order thinking. Here, I consider thinking as the sort of mental activity that uses facts to plan, order, and work toward an end, seeks meaning or an explanation, is self reflective, and uses reason to question claims, and make judgments. This seems to be what most teachers have in mind when they talk about thinking. For centuries,

many people have assumed that the study of certain subjects - such as algebra, Latin, and physics-have a desirable effect on the development of intellect. These subjects, it was thought, develop the mind such as a physical activity develops the muscles. John Dewey (1933/ 1971) rejected the view, writing, "It is desirable to expel the notion that some subjects are inherently intellectual and hence possessed of an almost magical power to attain the faculty of thought (p. 46).

Whenever a person is engaged in solving a problem, he/ she is engaged in a process. The process is to seek a solution to a dilemma. Thinking is involved in seeking an answer to a practical problem. Practicality is inherent when information gathered is used to solve an identified problem. Interest and effort are used to solve problems.

REFERENCES

Dewey, John (1933/1971), *How We Think.* Chicago. Henry Regnery (Original works published in 1933).

Ediger, Marlow (2007), "Learning Activities in the Curriculum," *College Student Journal,* 41 (4), 967-969.

Ediger, Marlow, and D. Baskara Rao (2007), *School Science Education.* New Delhi, India: Discovery Publishing House.

Ediger, Marlow (2007 b), "Meaning in Reading Instruction," *Reading Improvement,* 44(4), 2117-220.

Ediger, Marlow (2006), "Scaffolding and the Reading Curriculum," *Iowa Educational Leadership.* 8 (4), 24-26.

Noddings, Nel (2008), "All Our Students Thinking", *Educational Leadership,* 85 (5), 9-13.

14

Establishing Meaning in Science Curriculum

A meaningful science curriculum is important for students. If meaning is not present, students tend to feel that science consists of irrelevant subject matter. Rather facts, concepts, and generalizations achieved need to be understood and applied. A variety of learning opportunities may well assist students to attach meaning to ongoing lessons and units. They need to provide for individual differences as well as meet needs of learners. Pupils differ from each other in a plethora of ways including background information, abilities to learn, and interests, among others.

It behooves the science teacher to assist each pupil to achieve optimally. What might the science teacher do to assist pupils individually to learn as much as possible in the science curriculum?

Learning Opportunities to Achieve Objectives

Science experiments and demonstrations should be the heart of ongoing lessons and units of study. They must be challenging and engaging, and yet success in learning needs emphasis. Thus, developmental appropriate experiences are in the offing. To assist in meaningful learnings, with furniture arranged appropriately, the pupil needs to carefully observe the experiment/demonstration to notice what truly transpires. Careful planning is necessary to optimize learner achievement. Readiness for future experiences are based on previously acquired knowledge, and skills (Ediger and Rao, 2007).

For meaningful learning, the pupil and/or the teacher must determine contextually, the purposes of the experiment. A need should exist to set up the activity to enhance and develop indepth pupil learning. An hypothesis must be developed and tested. The hypothesis will be accepted, modified, or refuted. A new problem may arise within the bounds of attempting to solve a previously identified problem area.

Sometimes, the science teacher needs to scaffold ideas in order for the learner to achieve increasingly more complex facts, concepts, and generalizations. Scaffolding represents a gap between present learner achievement and a goal to attain. To realize the goal, the science teacher may specifically sequence subject matter so that it is attainable. Scaffolding is a valuable concept to use in teaching and learning situations since it stresses a gap to eliminate between the actual and the ideal in pupil learning. Committees may also be used to eliminate the gap. As peers discuss a problem area, they share ideas in moving toward the desired objective (Ediger, 2007).

Metacognition is also a valuable teaching concept. With metacognition, the learner engages in thinking about thinking. With teacher demonstration and assistance, the pupil may also reflect upon upon his/her thinking on how the problem was chosen for the science experiment. The steps in making the selection are pondered upon. Possibly, equally important is to reflect upon the processes involved in'developing an hypothesis. Both may be monitored by the learner in ensuing science lessons and units of study. By monitoring his/her progress, the pupil may make continuous progress in achieving developing, and growing. Each step in problem solving might well involve reflection and taking note of personal progress made. With metacognition, pupils perceive meaning and understanding in what was accomplished (Savithiri, 2006).

Pupils need to attach meaning in ongoing lessons and units of study. What is learned must make sense. Reading to solve identified problems in science frequently causes problems to the learner. Readiness for reading in an ongoing science lesson/unit of study needs to be emphasized. Thus, background information must be activated for the ensuing reading activity. This involves the following :

- discussing related illustrations in the science basal textbook or the library book.
- noticing carefully the new words, printed on the white board, contained in the ensuing lesson. These must be identified and pronounced accurately as well as used correctly in a sentence.
- selecting questions to be answered through reading. The questions might also expand into a problem solving experience, using a variety of reference sources.
- followup experiences after the reading experiences has been concluded such as using the information in discussions as well as in small group and committee work (Ness, 2007).

The above sequential steps emphasize that students attach meaning in what is being learned and acquired. Monitoring one's own progress makes certain that what is read is understood. If vocabulary terms cause difficulties, these need to be noted and gaps in their understanding minimized with appropriate activities. Pupils need to monitor their own reading progress in noticing adequacy in comprehension of content. Reflective thinking assists in ascertaining if the reading activity makes sense and is not mere word calling.

Meaningful learning may accrue through the use of a variety of learning activities. Concrete experiences include the use of objects, models and items in teaching and learning situations. Semi-concrete materials are one step removed from the concrete and include the use of illustrations, power point presentations, video-tapes, slides, specimens, pictures, single concept film loops, among others. Abstract materials include the use of printed materials, vocabulary charts, graphs, information in tabular form, word walls, audio recordings, among others, involving science subject-matter.

Methods of teaching used should engage pupils and provide for meaningful content. These include :

- learning by discovery in a hands on approach
- inductive procedures with heavy pupil involvement in ongoing science lessons and units of study
- project methods involving construction experiences
- deductive learnings presented by the science teacher/ peers
- large group, committees, and individual endeavors
- homogeneous as well as heterogeneous grouping depending upon involved purposes
- team teaching, use of learning centers, and non-graded science experiences
- constructivism within the curriculum (Sridevi, 2007).

Methods of instruction used need to assist pupils to achieve as optimally as possible. The science teacher must have high, reasonable expectations for each learner. Optimal achievement for each pupil is an ideal to strive toward.

Critical and Creative Thinking

Two kinds of thinking need differentiation in teaching pupils, namely critical and creative thinking. Critical thinking emphasizes separating facts from opinions, accurate from inaccurate content, as well as fantasy from reality. This type of thinking works well in science which is a an exacting body of knowledge. In comparison, creative thinking stresses innovative ways of doing things such as in problem solving. There are different ways to approach and solve a problem. For example, one familiar procedure emphasizes identifying a problem; developing an hypothesis; evaluating the hypothesis; and changing, modifying, or refuting the hypothesis, if necessary. Pupils need to reflect on how they solved problems. Methods used may be unique to the learner. However, objectivity is to be stressed strongly in all attempts to secure knowledge and skills in science.

Critical thinking stresses an objective stance in evaluating and accepting scientific knowledge. The personal feelings of the individual pupil are to be left out when acquiring subject matter in the earth, biological, and physical sciences in the school curriculum. This is the philosophy of realism which stresses that one can know the real world as it truly is, independent of the observer (Adams and Pierce, 2003).

An issue which continues to arise is attempts by school boards, among others, to bring in intelligent design as an alternative, to evolution, or part of the science curriculum. Backers of intelligent design have been well organized in their attempts to include their thinking into the science curriculum. Intelligent design emphasizes that a supreme being created the universe and its inhabitants. This point of view is not subject to scientific analysis. The methods of science stress that data be verifiable and objective. Since intelligent design does not meet the criteria for being included in science, it might come under the heading of theology which, among other things, deals with religious beliefs pertaining to the origin of the universe.

Science, too, stresses the use of the five senses-seeing, smelling, tasting, touching, and hearing-in the here and the now to obtain scientific subject-matter. Chemistry, for example, indicates the preciseness of measurable quantities such as in the Periodic Table of Elements. Thus, for example, water, contains two atoms of hydrogen and one atom of oxygen, expressed in a mathematical formula. Sense information in science, too, is extended through the use of scientific instruments such as microscopes, telescopes, and computer calculations, among others (Katz, February 16, 2008).

Self-efficacy in the Science Curriculum

Self-efficacy pertains to feelings about the self, such as adequate and possessing a good self concept. Science teachers need to possess self-efficacy. It is important that science teachers feel and believe that they can teach all pupils, effectively, to achieve well in the curriculum. Regardless of the following factors, self efficaciousteachers believe they can assist each pupil to achieve more optimally :

- socio-economic levels
- the home environment
- safety factors in the community (Bandura, 1997).

To possess much confidence in teaching science is salient. Teachers need to develop a good self concept by being proficient in scientific knowledge, particularly in subject-matter and processes taught to pupils. These feelings, no doubt, are revealed to learners in teaching and learning situations. Indepth knowledge and skills in science are needed. Ways of growing as a science teacher might well involve the following :

- taking course work in biology, physics, and chemistry, among others, to strengthen indepth understanding of subject matter.
- enrolling in university classes pertaining to methods of teaching science.
- reading professional literature in science and teaching methods such as Science and Children, and the Science Teacher, both published by the National Science Teachers Association (NSTA). Each school needs to

have a designated place in the library for teachers to read content from professional educational journals.

- attending state and national teacher education conventions, involving the teaching of science. In addition to the NSTA and state affiliated conventions, the Association for Supervision and Curriculum Development (ASCD) has annual conventions with sectional meetings dealing with the teaching of science, as well as teaching in general.
- writing manuscripts for publication in state and national teacher education journals. In gathering information for writing, the science teacher becomes increasingly knowledgeable of excellence in teaching.

By developing the self in subject-matter and methods of teaching science, self efficacy is being stressed. The teacher has a larger knowledge base to use in the science curriculum. He/she needs to lean upon the self to emphasize confidence in teaching pupils from diverse backgrounds of experience. A well prepared teacher might then have all the trappings which stress self efficacy in teaching. It also should assist, with multiple teaching strategies, to assist pupils to attach meaning in achieving objectives in ongoing science lessons and units of study.

REFERENCES

Adams, Cheryll M., and Rebecca L Pierce (20030, "Teaching by Tiering," *Science and Children*, 41 (3), 30-34.

Bandura, Albert (1997), *Self Efficacy: The Exercise of Control*, New York: W. H. Freeman.

Ediger, Marlow (2007), "Learning Activities in the Curriculum," *College Student Journal*, 41 (4), 967-969.

Ediger, Marlow, and D. Bhaskara Rao (2007), *School Science Education.* New Delhi, India: Discovery Publishing House.

Katz, Gregory (February 16, 2008), "Battle Over Evolution Flares Up in Europe," The Hutchinson, *Kansas News*.

Ness, Molly (2007), "Reading Comprehension Strategies in Secondary Content-Area Classrooms," *Phi Delta Kappan*, 89 (3), 229-231.

Savithiri, V. (2006), Impact of Metacognitive Strategies in Enhancing Perceptual Skills Among High School Students on Learning Geometry. Ph. D. thesis appraised by the writer for Alagappa University (India).

Sridevi, K. V. (2007), "Constructivism : A Shift in the Paradigm of Teaching-Learning Process," *Edutracks*, 7 (4), 9-13.

15

Assessment of Student Achievement in Science

There are a plethora of methods which are useful in evaluating student achievement in science. Mandated testing stresses the use of multiple choice test items to appraise learner progress. These are emphasized as being objective in that all students :

- take the same test for a particular grade level
- adhere to the same time limits in test taking
- receive the same directions for taking the test
- tests are machine scored, not subject to human error in scoring unless there are glitches (Toch, 2006).

Mandated tests generally have norms. Local test results are compared against these norms which indicate from pilot studies what average achievers for each grade level should accomplish. The only point at which there is human intervention is when specialists determine and write test items. Otherwise, there is strict objectivity, unless errors are made through machine scoring. Even in the case of selecting the multiple choice test items to be ordered and placed on the test, there is an objective way, called item analysis, in arranging the multiple choice test items from the easiest to the complex in ascending order of difficulty (Ediger and Rao, 2007).

Evaluating Student Achievement in Science

At the heart of teaching science, the teacher needs to emphasize conducting of experiments relating directly to the ongoing unit of study. Learners need adequate background information to understand meanings involved in conducting the experiment. Teacher observation is needed to ascertain how well the experiment is being conducted by students with teacher assistance. Involvement by each student is also necessary when suggesting outcomes (hypotheses) for the experiment. Careful observation by each student is needed when the actual experiment is being performed. There are selected observations which need appraisal by the teacher which standardized tests will not measure. First, the experiment is performed in context within a unit of study and is not an isolated episode as is true of paper/pencil tests. Second, readiness for conducting the experiment is a must in order that students attach meaning to the ongoing activity. In standardized testing, background information is not addressed. Third, the experiment represents reality. A paper/pencil test may have a drawing of a science experiment, .but actuality is missing. Then too, students work with objects in conducting an experiment; hands on approaches are lacking in test taking. Fourth, students see and observe an experiment; they do not merely respond to a test item. Fifth, students hypothesize the outcomes of the experiment. This salient item is lacking completely in testing situations (Adams and Pierce, 2003).

There are additional weaknesses in standardized testing including watching the excitement of an actual science experiment!

Mandated Tests and Reading Subject-matter

Mandated testing stresses reading about science; doing science is being minimized. Reading is done in mandated testing to fill in the bubble. The goals is to do well on a test whose results spread students from high to low based on the normal distribution curve. Results are determined from pilot studies in ascertaining rank of students having taken the test. Test result scores are generally provided in percentiles. They may range from the ninety ninth to the first percentile. Precise results in numerical terms are provided (Levin, 2007).

To be sure, teaching science does emphasize reading of subject matter, but is stressed along with experimentation. Science education does make its many contributions to reading across the curriculum. Thus to assist in confirming an hypothesis or extend learnings, students may read related selections from the basal, the internet, or other appropriate reference sources. The science teacher may also provide much assistance in word recognition and comprehension. Word recognition techniques useful in reading science content are the following :

- phonics in which there is consistency between letters and their respective sounds. There is a point of no return in teaching phonics when words lack consistency in spelling between symbol and sound.
- students lose interest in science learning due to drill on phonetic elements (Boyd-Batstone 2004).

The interests of students in science needs to be developed and maintained. Interest is a powerful factor in learning. To develop interest in reading science content for young learners and for struggling older readers, the writer recommends a large book approach. Thus, in relating reading of science content to experimentation, students may read using a Big Book approach. Here, the teacher needs to secure a library book, large enough for all to see clearly in a small group of six to seven students. The teacher needs to discuss the ^illustrations, first, pertaining to what will be read from the Big Book. Student readiness and attention needs to be obtained for and during the ensuing activity. Continuous teacher observation and evaluation are necessary. Quality criteria must be used in the asessment. Next, the teacher reads aloud the subject matter from the Big Book, as he/she points to the sequential words. This is followed with the science teacher reading aloud together with the involved students. The words are still pinpointed by the teacher as the activity progresses. This procedure may be repeated as often as necessary for learners to secure relevant science unit ideas (Ediger, 2007).

With the Big Book approach, pupils read ideas in an orderly way without hesitating on unknown words. With repeating the read aloud, learners reflect upon the basic sight vocabulary words attained and upon ideas read. When supervising university student teachers in the public schools, several teachers supervised by the writer used the Big Book approach in teaching. Understanding of subject matter is a key concept in teaching as well as developing sequential skills in reading. Vocabulary terms are generally defined when context clues are used since the surrounding words or paragraph assist in defining meaning of unknown words. Teacher self assessment is salient in teaching and learning situations, In assessing, the teacher, for example, must ask questions of the self, such as, "Are students on task in the ongoing lesson?"

Reading of science subject-matter related directly to the ongoing unit of study and to experimentation helps students to learn content in-depth as well as expand learnings. Teacher use of basal textbooks in science should also assist students to develop an interest in and an appreciation of the natural world. Current events discussions may further involve reading such as comprehension of news items as well as listening to broadcasts on radio and viewing events on television. Multiple senses should be used in gathering information. Current events emphasize many news happenings such as :

- volcanic eruptions
- sheet and gully soil erosion

- mud slides and avalanches
- floods, hail, cyclones, and hurricanes.

Students need to learn the scientific principles involved in these happenings. The questions of "why" and "how" of each need to be stressed and might well emphasize problem solving. Cause and effect thinking are important to incorporate in ongoing lessons and units of study. For each natural disaster, students also need to learn how different social and charitable groups assist in humanitarian work.

The class as a whole may be taught to initiate a new science unit whereby students, for example, view a video tape on the causes of volcanic eruptions. Small group endeavors might stress doing well planned science experiments. For example, a small group of learners may make a grassed waterway to prevent soil erosion. Bare top soil placed in a wooden box, two feet by three feet, needs to be seeded to grass. With a slope of the box, water may be sprinkled or poured very lightly on the grass covering of the soil. The run off may be caught at the end of the box showing the affects of soil erosion. A grassed waterway might then be made on the soil which leads excess poured water to go down the slope and off the enclosure without erosion occurring. Illustrations of all natural phenomenon mentioned above may be secured from basal texts, different reference books, and from the internet (Ediger, 2002).

Criteria for Successful Teaching in Science

The science teacher must possess guidelines for doing high quality teaching. Thus, the teacher needs to :

- provide for diverse styles of learning as well as different developmental levels of students with a variety of learning experiences.
- meet social needs by having students work together in committee settings.

- assist learners in having esteem needs fulfilled. They need to be rewarded for improved performance.
- help learners achieve sequential optimal progress.
- plan each lesson and unit of study carefully as well as thoughtfully.
- use feedback from student achievement to make ensuing plans for teaching and learning (See National Research Council, 1996).

REFERENCES

Adams, Cheryll M., and Rebecca L. Pierce (2003), "Teaching by Tiering," *Science and Children*, 41 (3), 30-34.

Boyd-Batstone, Paul (2004), Focused Anecdotal Records Assessment: A Tool for Standards Based, Authentic Assessment," *The Reading Teacher*, 58 (3), 230-239.

Ediger, Marlow (2007), "Learning Activities in the Curriculum," *College Student Journal*, 41 (4), 967-969.

Ediger, Marlow (2002), 'The Supervisor of the School," *Education*, 122 (3), 602-604.

Ediger, Marlow, and D. Bhaskara Rao (2007), *School Science Education*. New Delhi, India: Discovery Publishing House.

Levin, Ben (2007), 'The Failure of Failure," *Phi Delta Kappan*, 89 (3), 234-235.

National Research Center (1996), *National Science Education* Standards. Washington, DC: National Academy Press.

Toch, Thomas (2006), 'Turmoil in the Testing Industry," *Educational Leadership*, 64 (3), 53-57.

16

Motivating Student Learning in Science

Motivating students to learn can be highly challenging to teachers. Motivation in the science curriculum is no exception. Pupils come to the classroom with different interests; science may or may not be one of these but must be motivated. Those who have strong interests in science will generally possess a considerable amount of background information for an ensuing lesson or unit of study. Then too, there must be opportunities to learn science in the home and school environment. If a parent converses about science content in the home setting and is well versed in this area, the pupil will be able to develop better background experiences. The parents level of education helps or hinders pupil achievement. Children learn from their parents values as to the importance of science and other curriculum areas. There are a plethora of additional differences among learners to discuss, including abilities. It does say that pupils differ from each other in science achievement and yet the role of the teacher is to provide for optimal pupil growth and development (Ediger, 2007-2008).

Motivation in Science

The science teacher must keep in mind methods to use in getting pupils involved in science learning. From reading science journal articles, securing information from university level teacher education textbooks, discussions with other teachers on innovative methods of teaching, as well as attending professional meetings, teachers might well develop a repertoire of teaching skills in developing learner involvement in ensuing lessons and units of study. Securing wholehearted learner attention in teaching and learning situations is an ideal and necessary in goal attainment. A carefully selected experiment, which all in the classroom can view clearly, might well attain pupil attention (Ediger and Rao, 2007).

The science experiment provides pupil readiness for a discussion in identifying a problem as well as developing an hypothesis. With deliberation and thought, different reference sources may be analyzed to test the hypothesis. The hypothesis may be accepted as is, refuted, or modified. Another problem might well arise within a problem solving activity.

The science experiment should engage pupils in learning. It needs to emphasize on task behavior. The experiment may stress brain storming in developing an hypothesis, indepth thinking in evaluating the hypothesis, and flexibility in keeping an open mind of accepting, refuting, or modifying the hypothesis. The scientific method is being stressed here with objective thinking in science, one of the multiple intelligences emphasized by Gardner (1993).

A second kind of motivating science activity is a semi-concrete experience involving a power point presentation. A very interesting set of slides observed by the writer was provided in a power point presentation. This was stressed in "Birds of Prey." The audio facet was given by a speaker whose clear voice provided meaningful subject-matter. Sequential slides pictured eagles, hawks, and ospreys, among others. Distinguishing features of the category "Birds Of Prey," included a discussion of the following parts: the beak, claws, vision, wings, and basic configuration of each. It is highly salient that readiness is in evidence for each ensuing slide. The background information provides readiness for the new learnings. Jumping too far ahead of pupils with the new objective to be stressed makes for meaningless learning. Learners must understand what is taught, otherwise the ensuing subject matter will not be understood. Conversely, if the sequence is paced too slowly, repetitive statements will be made. Meaning theory is highly significant to emphasize in ongoing lessons and units of study (Hansen, 2003).

Questions raised during the "Birds of Prey" power presentation were the following :

- how can eagles fly at a very rapid speed (About 150 miles per hour) and still be accurate in capturing its prey?
- in addition to size, what other characteristics make for differences between eagles and hawks?
- how can eagles and hawks survive during the Arctic winter season?
- which habitats do ospreys live in? Which adaptive features do ospreys possess?

For the small group sessions, pupils with teacher guidance developed and followed criteria such as the following:

- each pupil participating, but no one dominating committee work.
- ideas presented during the discussion being clear and meaningful.
- subject matter discussed circulating among participants, not between a few individuals only.
- respect for the thinking of others being emphasized.
- questions from participants encouraged.

With stressing quality criteria for committee work, pupils are more likely to stay on the topic being discussed. Periodically, evaluation sessions are conducted to assist pupils to appraise themselves in terms of having followed the designated criteria. These provide opportunities to strengthen small group endeavors as well as assist in developing indepth knowledge and skills. Improved human relations also may be in evidence. Rudeness, belittling, talking down to others, and being biased have no roles to play in education, be it within a committee, whole class endeavors, hallways, and in society. Intimidation is also a negative behavior which must be eliminated. The intimidator believes he/she can bring others into submission with dogmatic behaviour. Committee members, rather, need to harmonize their roles into a group project. They need to take time, in a brain storming session, to list unhealthy behavior which impedes progress and growth in learning (Darsana, 2007).

A related audio-visual activity to the power point experience is a meaningful video tape. The writer supervised university student teachers covering a thirty year period of time. In one classroom, the student as well as cooperating teacher presented background information and showed a video-tape on natural disasters. The contents covered tornados, hurricanes, avalanches, mud slides, and volcanic eruptions. Movement and motion were involved in the video tape, as compared to still life in the power point presentation. Pupils raised a plethora of questions in this learning activity. Generally, the problem areas identified possible causes of each. Tornados had caused much destruction recently in the midwestern states. One set of pupils volunteered to do an art activity showing stages of tornado development with accompanying descriptions of each. The rest of the pupils were assigned to small groups to do an activity on the remaining types of natural disasters. For example, one committee chose to do a mural on mudslides, showing sequential stages of its actions. There was a considerable amount of motivation in pursuing these activities.

Third, so far learning activities discussed include the concrete with a science experiment and the semi-concrete with a power point/video-tape experience. Another kind of activity might stress a project method. The project method may emphasizes construction work, by an individual or within a small group setting. A project must have a purpose, accepted individually or collectively. Thus, a reason exists for its being constructed, involving a learning by doing procedure. Hands on work is salient for learners in an ongoing unit of study. Within a science unit, which are selected important projects undertaken by pupils with teacher guidance? Making a solar collector, developing electro magnets of different levels of magnetic attraction, constructing different models of soil slope to test for soil erosion under diverse environmental factors (barren soil, a grass cover, a grass waterway to slow down water flow), and/or building -terraces to prevent eroding conditions.

Once the purpose is accepted, then planning to do the details of the project is stressed. Careful planning is significant; shoddy, haphazard work is to be discouraged. Quality work is necessary to do things well. Learning and achievement stress the importance of doing quality work. Following the planning of the project, meticulous carrying out of the plans is an important step in a worthwhile endeavor. Good work habits need emphasis. Diligence and perseverance are needed to bring the project to fruition. Lastly, in the project method, good standards must be used to appraise the completed product. Pupils learn much in doing well by looking at the results of the completed project. Good evaluative standards stress strengths which need to be emphasized to achieve quality objectives in ongoing science lessons and units of study.

Pupils from other classrooms were invited to observe the completed projects and listen to a description of each. Several pupils chose to enter their projects in the school's annual science fair. Learning activities and experiences might well branch out to be observed by others as highly worthwhile science experiences (Ediger, 2006).

A fourth kind of learning activity might well involve reading in science. Materials read need to be on the developmental level of the learner. Success in learning then is more likely to occur as compared to reading subject matter whose meaning is not understood. A carefully chosen basal, as well as library books, may be used as reference sources. They shed light on relevant topics being pursued. For example, basals/library books might contain subject matter to do indepth learning on avalanches or earthquakes. They may also be used to begin a new unit of study. These books generally contain numerous illustrations pertaining to the lesson/unit being taught. They need to be discussed with learners prior to the ensuing reading lesson. During the discussion, pupils will tend to identify questions which they want to have answered from the ongoing reading. To assist in word recognition, possible new words may be printed on the white board for pupils to see and discuss prior to reading silently or orally. By doing this, the teacher helps pupils to read subject matter more fluently. Followup activities should include :

- discussion of content read to incorporate critical and creative thinking.
- determining solutions to additional questions and problems identified.
- putting information in chart form such as in narrative, flow, vocabulary, organizational, graphs and tables, and classification charts (Ediger, 2007).

IN CLOSING

A variety of rich learning experiences need to be in the offing for science students. They must be developmental appropriate and meet student needs. These experiences must motivate students to achieve as optimally as possible.

REFERENCES

Darsana, M. (2007), "Relationship Between Emotional Intelligence and Certain Achievement Facilitating Variables Of Higher Secondary School Students," *Edutracks*, 7 (4), 25-31.

Ediger, Marlow-(2007-2008), "Student Vocabulary Development in the Science Curriculum," *Connecticut Journal of Science Eduction*, 45 (1), 12-13.

Ediger, Marlow, and D. Bhaskara Rao (2007), *School Science Education*. New Delhi, India: Discovery Publishing House.

Ediger, Marlow (2006), "Innovations in Teaching Science," *Missouri Science News*, March, 2006, 30-31.

Ediger, Marlow (20007), "Meaning in Reading Instruction," *Reading Improvement*, 44 (4), 217-220.

Gardner, Howard (1993), *Multiple Intelligences: Theory into Practice*. New York: Basic Books.

Hansen, Laurie E. (2003), "Science in any Language," *Science and Children*, 41 (3), 35-39.

17

New Science Teacher in School Setting

The new science teacher needs monitoring to adjust well to the school setting. He/she must receive the assistance necessary to do well in science teaching. Feelings of uncertainty and anxiety need to be minimized as much as possible. The new teacher needs to be orientated to the school. How might the mentor/teacher relationship assist to make for a productive life in teaching and learning situations as a science teacher?

Mentoring and the New Science Teacher

The new science teacher must develop feelings of wanting to obtain needed knowledge about the local school and also about becoming a true professional. Thus, the mentor, among other things, may help the science teacher to :

- locate science equipment and materials
- know other teachers in the school setting
- find common supplies for use in teaching
- become familiar with the school library
- understand how the school schedule is organized

- know rules and regulations for mandated testing
- organize the classroom for science teaching (Wessler, 2008).

Having graduated from an accredited university, the science teacher is ready to pursue actual teaching experiences. In the pre-service experiences, the future teacher did indepth course work in science content involving earth, biological, and physical sciences. Applying the content areas, he/she engaged in pre-service experiences with public school students in observation of classroom activities pertaining to teaching and learning. Here, the regular teacher served as a role model and assisted the pre-service teacher in working with students individually as well as in small groups. These activities, for example, included students :

- designing and making posters involving conservation of natural resources
- reading science subject matter from the basal text
- assisting students in mastering vocabulary terms
- helping learners in peer committee discussions
- constructing a model soil conservation grassed waterway
- demonstrating a science experiment (Noddings, 2008).

The early field experiences provided readiness for student teaching. In student teaching, the future teacher experienced the entire scope and sequence of classroom teaching. Thus, he/she with cooperating teacher assistance did the following in student teaching :

- developed and introduced a science unit on "The Changing of the Earth's Surface" in large group instruction.
- organized followup small groups in extending topics presented in large group instruction such as (*a*) erosion

of top soil, (*b*) terracing (*c*) planting trees for wind breaks (*d*) and seeding grass.

- assisted pupils to develop individual projects based on the science unit title, such as locating and presenting information on a self-chosen topic, doing an art project, and making a model, among others, decided upon through teacher/pupil planning (Mesa *et al.* 2008).

To provide readiness for engaging pupils in each of the above named tasks, the student teacher and the cooperating teacher cooperatively showed and discussed a video tape dealing with changes occurring on the earth's surface including earthquakes, volcanic eruptions, tornados, as well as floods and mud slides. To work effectively in committees, pupils practiced using recommended guidelines for small group work. These include that every one participates actively, stays on the topic, gives everyone a chance to participate, and emphasizes politeness in ongoing experiences (Ediger, 2008).

There are different reasons why science teachers are successful as compared those who lack these traits. The personality of the teacher is important. Thus, the teacher needs to be kind and highly accepting of others. This is modeled in situations involving committee endeavours in science. Rudeness and being inconsiderate are not characteristics which are admired by others. Values possessed by the teacher may well make for a good teacher. Believing in hard work is a value and this guides teachers in teaching and learning situations. Pupils are then evaluated based on effort put forth such as in doing a science experiment. Slovenly, careless work is not tolerated, but the best needs to go into student endeavors. Science teachers must present models for learner emulation in personality development and values (well prepared and taught lessons) put forth. Good teaching, too, may be considered as being learned behavior. Here, the science teacher studies and practices quality teaching endeavors in each day of instruction. This approach may soon become habitual and provide exemplars of excellence in teaching (National Research Council, 1996).

According to Kennedy (2006), schools and districts can indeed improve teaching and they can do so in at least three different ways. They can improve the hiring procedures by reducing the time they spend on interviews and increasing the time they spend watching candidate videotapes. They can improve their professional development by reducing the money they spend on programmes that offer bromides and exhortations and increasing the money they spend on para-professionals and on programs that address the real nuts and bolts of teaching. And they can improve their standard operating procedures so that they stop interfering with good teaching and start facilitating it.

The important lesson here is to think not just about teacher quality but also on teaching quality. Teaching is inherently an unpredictable, complex enterprise. But we are making it far more unpredictable than it has to be with policies and practices that go in the way of high quality teaching and learning.

There may be students who do not achieve as optimally as they are capable and may be labelled as being under-achieves. Each student needs to achieve as optimally as possible. New science teachers need to possess vital guidelines which assist in teaching and learning situations. Kumar *et al.*, (2008) provide the following for assisting learners individually to attain as well as possible :

- provide consistent and constructive feedback
- give choices, focus on interests
- vary teaching styles to accommodate learning styles
- provide for active and experimental learning
- use mentorship and role models
- adopt education that is relevant and personally meaningful; an education that provides insight and self understanding
- have nurturing, affirming classrooms.

New science teachers then need guidance in providing the best science curriculum possible, using strategies of instruction which motivate each learner. Engaging students to achieve, develop, and grow in goal attainment is salient. Science learning activities need to be challenging and yet make for enjoyment in achieving knowledge, skills, and attitudinal objectives. Understanding new facts, concepts, and generalizations propels the student in wanting to learn with intrinsic motivation being in evidence. Purpose, or reasons for learning, increases the motivational level of the student in ongoing science lessons and units of study. Individual differences among students need adequate provision so that successful achievers in science is possible (Ediger, 2007).

The New Teacher in the Instructional Arena

With adequate background information at his/her disposal, the new science teacher generally needs gradual induction into the regular classroom. Depending upon the revealed capabilities in science teaching, the amount of mentor assistance will vary from teacher to teacher. The heart of the science curriculum is doing experiments. Students must be actively involved in science experimentation. Motivating learners in desiring to do experiments needs to be emphasized with interesting readiness experiences. Careful observation by all is salient when the experiment is ongoing. Learners need to develop and then test an hypothesis. Objective thinking from students is wanted. Extended learnings from the experiment include :

- reading from a variety of related sources, including the internet, to confirm or refute the findings.
- doing a research project such as using the project method to incorporate hands on learning approaches.
- writing up each experiment, using proper style and grammar which is appropriate for the developmental level of the student. A bound volume may be made of these write ups.

- observing and summarizing related video tapes with summarizing statements being placed in a student developed journal.
- working in a peer setting to summarize and assess several agreed upon library books on science directly related to the ongoing science unit of study.

IN CLOSING

Perhaps, the best way to conclude this manuscript is to quote the following criteria as to the main characteristics of science:

1. Science proceeds on the assumptions, based upon centuries of experience, that the universe is not capricious.
2. Science knowledge is based on observation of samples of matter that are accessible to public investigation in contrast to purely private inspection.
3. Science aims at achieving a systematic and comprehensive understanding of various sectors or aspects of nature.
4. Science is not, and probably never will be a finished enterprise and there remains very much more to be discovered about how things in the universe behave and how they are inter-related.
5. Measurement is an important feature of most branches of modern science because of the formation as well as the establishment of laws facilitated through the development of quantitative distinctions (Seeniammal, 2007).

REFERENCES

Ediger, Marlow (2008), "The School and Students in Society," *Journal of Instructional Psychology*, 35 (3), 260-263.

Ediger, Marlow (2007), *Science Curriculum and Instruction*. New Delhi, India: Discovery Publishing House.

Kennedy, Mary M. (2006), "From Teacher Quality to Teaching Quality," *Educational Leadership*, 63 (6), 14-19.

Kumar, M. Suresh, et. al. (2008), Reversing the Underachievement of School Students through Motivational Strategies," *Edutracks*, 8 (2) 16-17. Published in India.

Mesa, Jennifer C. *et al.* (2008), "The P.O.E.T.R.Y Of Science," *Science and Children*, 46 (3), 36-41.

National Research Council (1996), *National Science Education Standards*, Washington, DC: National Academy Press.

Noddings, Nel (2008), "Schooling for Democracy," *Phi Delta Kappan*, 90 (1), 34-37.

Seeniammal, V. (2007) A Study of Problems of High School and Higher Secondary School Students in Learning Chemistry in Tirunelveli District, Ph D thesis appraised by the writer for VOC College of Education, Centre for Research in Education, Tamil Nadu, India (page 6) with recognition for. these'standards going to The National Science Teacher's Association, Washington, DC.

Wessier, Stephen (2008), "Civility Speaks Up," Educational Leadership 66 (1), 44-48.

18

Mentoring and Science Teacher

The mentor is one who is highly knowledgeable about science content as well as methods of teaching. He/she is able to work effectively and well with others. The mentor is able to motivate science teachers to teach students to achieve more optimally, using a variety of recommended approaches.

Mentoring is a procedure which, among others, helps teachers in inservice education and to update teaching methods in science. Quality science teaching needs to be emphasized and continuous growth is necessary.

Science teachers need to develop a philosophy of instruction which which provides direction in teaching and learning. There are theories of learning which provide guidance involving the teacher in making curricular decisions. Science teachers need to model that which is objective and truly independent of any observer. Objectivity, among other facets, then is a key element to stress in teaching science. Teachers with a rich, solid base of science content have more to offer than isolated facts. The base is useful in guiding students to develop functional concepts, generalizations, main ideas and applicable skills (Ediger and Rao, 2007).

The Science Teacher in the Mentoring Process

Mentors need to possess a nourishing and professional relationship with science teachers. He/she needs to possess the knowledge, skills, and attitudes to assist science teachers in continual growth and achievement in the teaching/learning processes. What roles do mentors play in efforts at curriculum improvement?

The methods of science need much emphasis in the curriculum. Careful observation, inquiry methods, and problem-solving are major goals to stress. Individuals live in a world of science with rapid inventions in the area of technology. Scientists have provided the latest technology to improve the human condition. Labour saving devices have made the world of work easier and more efficient. Medical science has provided better health practices and care among humans. Many deadly diseases of the past are no longer a major threat such as polio, diphtheria, and cholera. With a longer life span, individuals experience an increase in cancer, heart attacks, strokes, and diabetes. New threats in bacterial and viral mutations do make for ensuing threats to human health. In addition to labor saving devices, as well as better health care and life expectancy, Agricultural and food supplies have increased in productivity. Supermarkets abound in food products and for many people, obesity is a problem. The writer taught on the West Bank of the Jordan for two years and observed bedouins (nomads) frequently. Bedouins are very slender, living in harsh conditions in a desert setting with food being in extremely short supply. There are no problems with obesity in bedouin life observed (Ediger, 2007).

The objectives for student attainment need to be clarified so that definite goals are to be achieved by learners. They need to be set at a level which are developmentally appropriate for students. Objectives which are too difficult may well lead to frustration or student failure. Toward the other extreme, Relatively easy objectives to attain might lead to boredom. With clarified objectives, it is necessary to align learning activities with these chosen ends of instruction.

The learning activities need to engage learners in ongoing lessons and units of study. These include individual and small group experiences such as the following :

- reading from the science basal text, library books, science encyclopaedias, as well as needed information from the internet.
- emphasizing project methods which relate to the ongoing science lesson/unit of study.
- engaging in problem-solving experiences which involve a problem, an hypothesis, and a tentative conclusion, subject to further testing.
- taking excursions, as well as doing journal writing, diary entries, and note taking.
- making models pertaining to concepts and generalizations studied in science (National Science Education Standards, 1996).

Performing science experiments is the heart of the science curriculum. Throughout each of the above asterisked items, a related experiment may be conducted. If possible, safe, and developmentally appropriate, students should be involved in doing the experiment. Carefully planned and initiated, each experiment should be clearly visible to learners. There must be a purpose for each science experiment and that being to make a concept/generalization meaningful to students. It is a vital approach in teaching and is central to science learnings. Student interest in science may certainly be stimulated with quality experiments. Processes used in science should assist students to make valid predictions, accurate observations, make good inferences, classify information, as well as communicate effectively. Students should also learn to ask quality questions, visualize subject matter, and summarize information obtained. It is salient for learners to make connections with the science subject matter acquired by making use of what has been learned. Relating content presently learned to subject matter previously acquired assists in integrating and retaining ideas (Fitzhugh, 2006).

Higher Levels of Cognition

Mentors need to help science teachers guide students to do more intensive thinking. This means that indepth learning will be fostered regardless of the learning activity pursued in ongoing lessons and science units of study. Analytic thinking is highly useful to emphasize. Here, the student is guided to separate facts from opinions, accurate from inaccurate statements, as well as fantasy from reality. Objective thinking is then being stressed. A synthesis of thought should occur after analyzing content being studied. Problem-solving, for example, emphasizes that students synthesized information in order to secure an hypothesis or tentative answer. Also, project methods stress the importance of integrating science subject matter in order to engage in making models and doing construction work.

Science teachers need to assist students to reflect upon what has been learned. Thus after reading science subject matter, the student mentally rethinks what has been read and might well answer the following questions :

- which major ideas did I comprehend?
- how did the related illustrations assist in understanding what was read?
- in the large and small group discussions, which ideas were clarified from my reading of information?
- how did the internet help to secure additional information?
- what would I like to learn which was not covered in the above named questions (Ediger, 2007)?

The science teacher must learn to use metacognition strategies in teaching and learning situations. Thus, he/she rehearses what was taught with the intent of improving over previous times. The teacher views what might have been changed to :

- secure more wholehearted involvement of learners in the ongoing lesson in science.
- develop student learnings more indepth pertaining to specific identified concepts.
- improve student sequence in learning.
- assist learners to understand identified vital vocabulary terms.

Evaluation of Achievement

Mentors have much responsibility in assisting science teachers in appraising student achievement. The appraisal results should provide feedback to the teacher in assisting learner achievement. Teacher observation of students is one significant procedure. Here, the teacher must use proper criteria in the evaluation process. These criteria may be inherent in the following by assessing :

- portfolios developed by pupils of representative work in ongoing science units of study.
- on task behavior in ongoing science lessons.
- student responsibility for completing and doing well in assigned activities.
- learners being meticulous in processes involving the project method.
- active participation of students in small and large discussion groups.
- scientific journals kept of investigations and experiments conducted in the classroom and home setting (Barclay et.al., 1999).

Pertaining to Scientific Journals, Beckstead (2008) wrote:

Because every writing assignment occurred at the end of a science unit and required inclusion of scientific concepts covered in the unit, our scientific journals were an excellent form of assessment. Through these types of writing, a teacher can learn many things about the student's understanding of the concepts covered in a unit of study. By reading a student's essay, poem, or letter, the teacher can determine if a student needs clarification of any misconceptions they may have. These articles also help a teacher determine if a concept needs to be re-taught...

Evaluation is an important responsibility of the science teacher. The teacher must use quality procedures to ascertain how well each student is doing in science. Instruction might well improve by using feedback from evaluation results. Metacognition is then involved.

IN CONCLUSION

The mentor has salient responsibilities in developing quality science teachers. These teachers need to have adequate knowledge and skills pertaining to selecting objectives, learning activities, and evaluation procedures in ongoing science units of study.

REFERENCES

Barclay, D. (1999), Making the Connections: Science and Literacy," *Childhood Education*, 75 (3), 146-152.

Beckstead, Larissa (2008), "Scientific Journals," *Science and Children*, 46 (3), 22-26.

Ediger, Marlow, and D. Bhaskara Rao (2007), *School Science Education*. New Delhi, India: Discovery Publishing House, p.5.

Ediger, Marlow (2007),"Teacher Observation to Assess Student Achievement," *Journal of Instructional Psychology*, 34 (1),137-139.

Ediger, Marlow (2007), "The Substitute Teacher in Reading Instruction," *The SubJournal*, 8 (2), 67-73.

Fitzhugh, Will (2006), "Where's the Content?" *Educational Leadership*, 64 (2), 42-47.

National Science Education Standards (1996), *National Research Council*. Washington, DC: National Academy Press.

19

Substitute Teacher in Science

Too frequently when the regular teacher is absent due to illness or bereavement in the family among other reasons, students in the classroom are taught by someone poorly prepared for teaching-science. The term "baby sitting" is generally applied to these situations. Must it be that way? The answer is a resounding "no!" School districts need to provide paid inservice education for those desiring to substitute teach in science. When absences occur of the regular teacher, the substitute teacher needs to play the role of a qualified science teacher in assisting students to achieve as optimally as possible. Sequence in student science achievement is hindered with substitute teachers who merely are present in the classroom and do not engage learners in ongoing lessons and units of study (Ediger, 2007).

Inservice Education and the Substitute Teacher

The substitute teacher needs assistance from a lead teacher or science supervisor to be fully cognizant of the duties and responsibilities of teaching science. The basal science textbook, the course of study, lesson plans, and designed units of study, along with being introduced to the materials of instruction, provide a basis for the inservice education programme (Ediger, 2007).

The subteacher needs orientation as to what is the heart of the science curriculum, namely experimentation. He/she should observe how experiments fit into each lesson/unit of study. Experimentation is integrated, not a separate entity. Prior to an experiment, students need to possess adequate readiness to benefit from the learning activity. Looking at and discussing a related videotape will assist in providing readiness in that necessary knowledge and skills are then activated (National Research Council, 1996).

Students need to observe the experiment carefully and not jump to hasty conclusions. Objective information is a requirement. Opinions and subjective ideas are treated as hypotheses and are tested in the experiment. Results from the experiment are corroborated/refuted with additional research. The one variable, alone, must be tested in the experiment. Extraneous factors need to be eliminated. The subteacher, too, needs to be highly knowledgeable of data sources to check the results of an experiment or to extend knowledge about related concepts and generalizations. These include the following using :

- internet and world wide web sources.
- up to date trade books, basal science series, and science encyclopedias.
- DVDs containing relevant and reliable information.
- information from a nearby university science professor or other science teachers in the school setting.
- a redoing of the original experiment (Wenglinsky, 2006).

The subteacher needs to understand what is meant by learnings being developmentally appropriate for a student.

Quality sequence is not possible in teaching and learning situations unless the activities and experiences are challenging and yet optimal achievement is possible. With high expectations for each student and success in learning being in evidence, the science teacher might well feel successful in teaching. Student learning and understanding is attached to what is being learned. It is highly significant for students to perceive purpose in learning. Reasons for active involvement in ongoing lessons and units of study are then being stressed. The science teacher may state a purpose or students, periodically, may brainstorm reasons for participating in an ongoing topic. Thus, purposes should exist for student participation in :

- a problem solving activity such as in an experiment. The problem, an hypothesis, and a conclusion must be garnered by students with teacher guidance.
- a project method which involves student cooperative planning with teacher assistance. The project may, for example, deal with research on alternative sources of energy or how a home/school may conserve on energy consumption.
- a construction activity which night even provide an example for a local science fair (Zales and Unger, 2008).

Additional Needs of the Subteacher

The subteacher must be conscious of reading needs of students in in ongoing science lessons. These needs pertain to :

- word recognition assistance
- comprehension strategies with cause/effect as well as a critical and creative reading emphasis

Evaluation needs to be continuous using teacher observation, teacher written tests with appropriate validity and reliability, and performance tasks being stressed (Ediger, 2007).

IN CLOSING

Subteachers need to provide a quality science curriculum with the best objectives, learning activities, and appraisal techniques being used. High, reasonable expectations for student achievement need to be in the offing. Each student must achieve optimally in science!

REFERENCES

Ediger, Marlow (2007), *School Science Education.* New Delhi, India: Discovery Publishing House.

Ediger, Marlow (2007), "Learning Activities in the Curriculum," *College Student Journal*, 41 (40, 967-969.

Ediger, Marlow (2007), "The Substitute Teacher in Reading Instruction," *SubJournal*, 8 (2), 67-73.

National Research Council (1996), *National Science Education Standards.* Washington, DC: National Academy Press.

Wenglinsky, Harold (2005-2006), "Technology and Achievement : The Bottom Line," *Educational Leadership*, 63 (4), 29-33.

Zales, Charlotte Rapper, and Connie W. Linger (2008), "The Science and Literacy Framework," *Science and Children*, 46 (3), 42-45.

20

Assessing in Science Using Teacher Observation

Science teachers need to be very versatile in using diverse methods to ascertain pupil achievement and progress. These should be based on recommended criteria for learning in science. Quality science teaching should be an end result. Thus, feedback is provided to the teacher, based on evaluation results, as to what pupils have left to learn; it may also be used diagnostically to notice weaknesses in learning which need remediation. There are recommended methods to use in assessing learner progress. Major focus will be given to teacher observation (Ediger 2007).

Methods of Assessment

Teacher observation of pupil achievement might well be an excellent way of noticing science achievement. Here, the science teacher must focus upon salient pupil learnings which are necessary to help pupils develop efficacy in knowledge, skills, and attitudes. Here, the science teacher models and helps the learner to attend carefully to ongoing science experiences. Objective thinking, inquiry learning, and developing quality attitudes toward learning may also be modeled, and noticed if achieved, through teacher observation. Pupils need to become increasingly proficient in these areas.

It is difficult to test pupils to notice achievement in selected areas such as in doing objective thinking, engaging in inquiry learning, as well as becoming efficacious in doing well in performing experiments. Thus, teacher observation might provide important needed information on learner progress. A set of pupils, for example, may be observed in the following :

- how carefully an experiment was designed and carried out
- how meticulous pupils stated an hypothesis
- how the hypothesis was tested and appraised
- how the tentative hypothesis was modified if need be (National Science Education Standards, 1996).

If a team of teachers is evaluating pupils pertaining to the above named criteria, they might compare their individual appraisal results to notice consistency from one rater to the next on a five point scale. One being the lowest and five being the highest rating. Consistency among raters improves the reliability of the raters. The science teacher individually or the team collectively should look at the results and notice where assistance needs to be given to shore up improved teaching and learning. If hypothesis development, for example, is the weakest, then ample opportunities must be presented to help pupils develop more proficiency in this area. Since experimentation is the heart of the science curriculum, it is salient to gather information on how successful each activity is in helping pupils secure needed facts, concepts, and generalizations as well as involved processes within an ongoing lesson or unit of study.

Teacher observation of process and product appraisals may be acquired in many facets of learning in the science curriculum such as in the project method. Pupils, for example, making a chart showing predator/prey relationships, may show illustrations and a brief summary of each involved vertebrate—fish, amphibians, reptiles, birds, and mammals. Accurate and complete information needs to be given each accompanying illustration. For a cooperative enterprise, the science teacher needs to consider the following in teacher observation to assess pupil progress :

- each pupil participating actively, but not dominating the experience
- positive relationships among peers in the ongoing project
- encouragement and acceptance of each person's contributions
- neatness in the completed project
- self evaluation in terms of desired criteria (Ediger, 2008).

The above-named criteria must be discussed prior to and during the time the project is being emphasized. By following desired standards, the committee will tend to develop a better chart.

Quality teacher observation, also, is salient to stress when learners are involved in teacher or peer lead discussions in a relevant science lesson. Criteria such as the following may be developed by the science teacher or cooperatively with pupils :

- pupils stay on the topic being discussed.
- pupils interact effectively with each other when presenting ideas as in being polite and accepting of each other.
- pupils reveal understanding of ideas presented.
- pupils present content sequentially (See Olson, 2008).

Feedback from pupils provide learning activities to be used in diagnosis and remediation. Thus, if pupils are weak in presenting content sequentially, the science teacher may model an example of good versus inadequate sequence. By using one or more models provided by the science teacher, pupils should grasp what is meant by having quality sequence within a discussion. Discussions, too, like many learning activities may be evaluated on a five point scale. Selected teachers and supervisors desire to use a rubric in the evaluation process. Thus, a rubric contains standards from five being the highest to one being the lowest in quality of work performed by students. A rating of five might well indicate excellent work, a rating of four superior work, a rating of three average achievement, a rating of two being below average, and a rating of one "needs improvement," from the above list of four asterisked items pertaining to pupil participating in discussions. The pupil's name must appear on the rubric. Much valuable information may be secured from the rubric pertaining to assisting pupils to achieve vital objectives in discussions, as well as in other categories of science progress such as pupil achievement in problem solving. Vygotsky (1978) advocated that pupils work in committees since learning accrued when the ideas of peers "bounce of their minds" and provide for higher levels of thought.

Anecdotal statements, also, might well be used in the appraisal process. This devise stresses that the science teacher record observations made pertaining to a specific learner. Each observation is dated and as time goes on reviewed to notice a pattern of pupil behavior or used for diagnostic/remediation purposes. Observations made need to be recorded at the perceived time. Thus for a series of dated observations, a pupil, for example, revealed the following behaviors:

- September 30. Bill is quick in choosing a project to complete. However, his project on "Prehistoric Life" in diorama form did show thought in its selection
- October 15. Bill stayed on task, but could do neater work. The Tyrannosaurs Rex lacked proper proportion, although the prehistoric plants in the background were planned more carefully.

- November 6. Bill developed criteria for project evaluation such as neatness, accuracy, and thoroughness.
- November 10. Bill indicated he had done his best in doing the project, realizing he enjoyed art work. (Maheshwari, 2008).

By reflecting upon the anecdotal statements, the science teacher felt Bill tried hard to come up with a quality product, but needed assistance in being accurate and showing good workmanship. Information from the anecdotal statement was used in a conference with the involved pupil. As a result, the science teacher felt that Bill was paying more attention to improving both product and process in science. Anecdotal statements need to be written clearly and concisely so that the teacher may attach meaning to what needs to be emphasized in ensuing lessons and units of study (Costa, 2008).

Anecdotal statements may also be used to appraise learner achievement in written work such as in a report on reading a science library book related to the ongoing unit of study. Pupils individually may select the library book of their choosing, using the following standards in the written product :

- Main ideas were chosen from the library book contents with supporting ideas developed
- Details were utilized to substantiate the supporting ideas
- Vocabulary used was meaningful to the reader
- Order of sentences in the report was commendable
- Summary statements in the report included a holistic review of included subject-matter.

The report may be written in longhand with neatness/ legibility required, or with the use of the word processor. The latter is highly recommended if available and if the pupil, possesses needed skills in developing a quality document.

Quality oral communication, too, is vital. It is salient for each pupil to be able to convey science content to others so that understanding becomes paramount. Appropriate stress, pitch, and juncture may be modeled by the science teacher, prior to pupils presenting subject matter orally. Pupil enthusiasm is important in any science activity participated in. Science experiments, project methods, and problem solving experiences, among others, emphasize the importance of quality oral communication to convey information. Ketch (2006) wrote :

> In some classrooms, students are required to be quiet mosl of the day. They have little opportunities to practice thinking strategies or show evidence of their levels of cognitive development . . . Teachers who model cognitive strategies and foster student discussions know that strategies get better as students practice their use. In addition, teachers recognize the value in providing time for students to reflect, form ideas, cite evidence of their evolving thinking, and comprehend. Students involved in the conversation process can, over time, become reflective, critical thinkers.

REFERENCES

Costa, Arthur (2008), "The Thought-filled Curriculum," *Educational Leadership*, 65 (5), 20-25.

Ediger, Marlow (2007), *School Science Education.* New Delhi, India: Discovery Publishing House.

Ediger, Marlow (2008), "Leadership in the School Setting," *Education*, 129 (1), 17-20.

Ketch, Ann (2006), "Conversation: The Comprehension Connection," *The Reading Teacher*, 59 (1), 8-13.

Maheshwari, Amrita (2008), Integral Values of Science Education," *Edutracks*, 8 (4), 16-17.

National Science Education Standards. *National Research Council.* Washington, DC: Academy Press.

Olson, Joanne (2008), "Making Time for Science," *Science and Children*, 46 (3), 50-53.

Vygotsky, Len S. (1978), *Mind in Society: The Development of Higher Psychological Processes.* Cambridge Massachusetts: Harvard University Press.

21

Portfolios in Science

There are a plethora of methods which may be used to appraise pupil achievement in science. Portfolios are a significant approach. They may contain a representative sampling of actual pupil work in science. Teacher guidance is needed in developing the pupil portfolio. Pupils may use the portfolio to review what has been learned. Parents may also perceive what their offspring has learned in science units of study by looking at and asking questions about pupil performance. Among other times, this may occur at parent/teacher conferences. Here questions might be asked and answers clarified about a child's performance in science (Ediger, 2006).

Philosophy of Portfolio Use

Portfolios emphasize constructivism as a philosophy of instruction and evaluation. What is salient to learn is not measurable in many situations including motivation and attitudes within a specific science unit of study. The whole child is involved in learning such as the intellectual, the physical, the attitudinal, as well as the social dimension. More than specific parts of the learner are inherent in that various areas of growth and development are involved in achievement. Constructivism stresses open-ended objectives which provide flexible means of teaching and leave considerable leeway for pupil input. Thus, pupils have more control of their very own learning than is true of many classrooms. Evaluation tends to be more subjective as compared to using measurement procedures to assess pupil progress. Self evaluation by the pupil with teacher guidance is also emphasized (Ediger, 2007).

Constructivism stresses that pupils largely develop their own understandings with the assistance of the teacher. Motivational learning activities then need to be in the offing. Problem-solving experiences in context are encouraged. Pupil curiosity in ongoing science units encourages learners to ask questions and identify problem areas. A variety of reference sources are used to secure information whereby an hypothesis is developed and tested. Science experiments and demonstrations need to be incorporated as sources of information as well as being the heart of problem solving activities. The internet also provides valuable information as well as the more traditional procedures such as science textbook use, science encyclopedias, library books, and resource people who specialize in the knowledge being sought by pupils (National Research Council, 1996).

To constructionists, knowledge is not learned for its own sake, but it is to be used in functional situations such as to solve problems as well as to engage in project methods of achievement. It is not learned separate from skills since knowledge is to be applied. The level of application is very salient and it does eliminate/minimize what the student perceives as having little value or worth. Knowledge, too, is viewed as wholistic, rather than as separate subjects/components or categories to be mastered. A well balanced curriculum of subject matter (science, mathematics, social studies, and the language arts), as well as the fine/practical arts, and health and physical education are to be experienced by learners. Then too, personality development is salient including quality ethics, caring for others, assisting people, and as well as good attitudes in general (Beckstead, 2008).

Constructivism then stresses students developing a portfolio of randomized products showing what has been learned within a given period of time. The following may then become a vital part of a student's portfolio :

- a comprehensive write up of science experiments and demonstrations
- electronic photos of art work, murals, models, and committee work participated in ongoing science units of study
- essays, poems, summaries, and book reports written as a part of different science lessons/units of study
- recordings of oral book reports and summaries of concluded science learnings (Rose, 1999).

Testing to Notice Student Progress in Science

As compared to constructivism, testing stresses measurability of learner achievement. Thus, it can be measured to show quantitatively learner progress in diverse academic disciplines, including science. With quantitative data, students may be compared against each other in terms of achievement. The comparisons then reveal percentile differences among learners. A student may be on the 75th percentile, meaning out of every 100 students tested, 75 were below the 75th percentile. Or if a student was on the fiftieth percentile, out of every 100 tested, 50 students were above and fifty below the fiftieth percentile. E.L. Thorndike (1874-1949) stated basic beliefs pertaining to the measurement movement, "Anything that exists, exists in some amount, and if it exists in some amount, it can be measured." Questions arise pertaining to the following being measurable :

* caring for and assisting others as needed
* humanitarian feelings (Wolk, 2008).

Standardized tests for attitudes, for example, toward science or other academic disciplines have a rather low rating for reliability, This means that these kinds of tests dp not measure in a reliable manner. Thus, a student may take a test over again and the results may differ considerably from the first to the second time of testing. A highly reliable test has high correlations between alternate forms of a test, split half reliability, or test/retest reliability.

Standardized tests developed by a commercial company and, generally, for a specific age or grade level :

- contain clear directions for test taking
- specific time limits for test taking
- the same key used for computerized scoring of all tests
- mass numbers of tests scored with modern technology.

Testing is to be objective and free from opinions and biases. The only variable in testing situations is the individual student and his/her knowledge of subject matter. All other conditions are kept constant. In the case of mandated objectives, additional criteria for standardized tests include the following :

- pilot studies having been run to ascertain validity and reliability
- student results given in quantitative terms such as percentiles and/or grade equivalents
- norms provided to indicate where one's own students are achieving in relationship to those quantified from the pilot studies (Ediger, 2008).

CONCLUSION

Regardless of the teaching philosophy emphasized, the science teacher needs to provide pupils with interesting goal centered experiences. He/she also needs to :

- assist learners to be actively engaged in learning
- help pupils perceive meaning in learning
- motivate pupils to achieve, grow, and develop, in ongoing science units of study
- guide learners to experience purpose in learning.

REFERENCES

Beckstead, Larissa (2008), "Scientific Journals: A Creative Assesment Tool," *Science and Children*, 46 (3), 22-26.

Ediger, Marlow (2006), "Testing Versus Portfolios to Assess Achievement," *OASCD Journal*, 13 (1), 31-32.

Ediger, Marlow (2007), *School Science Education*. New Delhi, India: Discovery Publishing House.

Ediger, Marlow (2008), "Leadership in the School Setting," *Education*, 129 (1), 17-20.

National Research Council (1996), *National Science Education Standards.* Washington, DC: National Academy Press.

Rose, M. (1999), "Ten Easy Writing Lessons That Get Kids Ready for Writing Assessments". New York: Scholastic.

Wolk, Steven (2008),"Joy in School," *Educational Leadership*, 66 (1), 8-14.

22

A Stimulating Science Vocabulary Environment

Student interest in science may be extended through a rich vocabulary environment. Students need to see words and experience them in an interesting way. A variety of approaches need to be emphasized for students to see words in print and relate them to the concrete (objects and items used in teaching science) as well as the semi-concrete (illustrations, pictures, and pictorial representations of reality). Words are abstractions which convey and communicate ideas. A rich speaking, reading, writing, and listening vocabulary should assist students to become increasingly science literate (Zales and Unger, 2008).

Extending Student Learnings in Science

The interests of students need to be piqued in ongoing lessons and units of study in science. A variety of rich experiences must be in the offing which provide for students of diverse achievement levels. One procedure to set up a word wall in the classroom. When interesting new words are identified by students in discussion settings, they need to be printed, large enough for all to see clearly, and placed on the word wall. The writer when supervising university student teachers frequently noticed how learners congregate at the word wall, point to, and discuss meanings of these words. The content for discussion may have come from reading subject matter in the basal text. Words tend to fascinate students and encourage interesting comments and use (Ediger, 2007). How might these words be used?

With readiness involved, several students wrote different types of poetry which included rhymed verse such as couplets, triplets, quatrains, and limericks. A few wrote poems containing syllabication such as haiku and tankas. Still others wrote free verse and diamontes. Students had studied each of these kinds of poems previously in the language arts and were enthused in using science words in a creative manner. They also noticed the science/language arts connection.

Pupils being actively involved in sustained silent reading (SSR) was also observed in student teaching by the writer. Here, pupils chose science information and science fiction library books for the self selected reading activity. Generally, pupils choose library books written on their individual reading level. Pupil were encouraged to do more voluntary reading and in this case science library books. It is difficult to say how much increase in science knowledge accrued in SSR, but the writer feels there is much to gain in subject matter content, skills, and especially attitudes in a voluntary reading activity. Not all achievement is measurable; some must probably be inferred through rational judgement (Ediger, 2007).

The SSR is quite open ended in terms of being sequential learning experiences. Pupils must make many decisions on their very own in terms of which ordered books to read and quality comprehension which is desired from learners. Scaffolded Silent Reading (ScSSR) is more structured with the science teacher assisting in library book selection. When pupils read silently the chosen library book, the teacher randomly asks learners questions covering subject matter read. This is done to evaluate comprehension of science content. A pupil may also be asked to read a short selection aloud to appraise word recognition and fluency in reading.The teacher jots down a few observations made, dated, and with the pupil's name attached (Reutzel *et al.*, 2008). Progress in securing science facts, concepts, and generalizations is then noted for each pupil.

With either SSR or ScSSR, the involved pupil may keep a vocabulary notebook containing what he/she perceives to be important vocabulary terms. In small group sessions or the class as a whole, pupils may share recorded words. Growth in science vocabularies may occur through word walls and summaries of SSR/ScSSR library book reading. Both are available for review and study. It is good to rehearse science words and vocabulary terms to improve retention as well as interest.

Journals need to be kept by pupils of science experiments performed. One part of the write-up for each experiment should be devoted to science terminology used in the activity. Each experiment needs to be clearly visible and meaningful to all in the small group as well as those taught in large group instruction. Digital pictures need to be taken of different experiments and be a related part of the write-up. Illustrations may also be drawn by pupils to accompany an experiment. Journal entries need to pinpoint key vocabulary terms used (Alien, 2008).

A variety of rich experiences in ongoing science lessons and units of study aids pupils in securing relevant vocabulary terms which are useful presently as well as in the future. Thus, diary entries written by individuals or committees of significant learnings assist pupils to master vocabulary words. Alternating as to who writes the entries stimulates interest and avoids repetition and boredom. Sequential improvement in all written work is to be expected, using complete sentences, clarity of ideas, and variety in words as well as types of sentences used (National Research Council, 1996).

Words are powerful and can be use in a plethora of ways. Pertaining to the power of words, Wessler (2008) wrote the following:

> Words are central tools of education. Whether written or spoken, words can elucidate, inform, and inspire. But they can also scare, humiliate, and disempower. Degrading slurs, jokes,and epithets are pervasive in the hallways, cafeterias, buses, locker rooms, and even classrooms of middle and high schools everywhere.
>
> A school where degrading language slurs and jokes are widely used and rarely challenged is a place where violence is far more likely to occur. Some students will take the silence of bystanders as license to escalate their behavior from words to harsher words, threats, and finally violence. In every instance of violence that I have investigated in schools, first as a hate crime prosecutor and more recently when administrators asked me to help them respond to serious misconduct, I have seen this same process of escalation.

The above quote pin-points the positive as well as the negative use of words. A positive classroom environment stresses the importance of using words to achieve, grow, and develop on the part of students and teachers. A threatening, negative classroom environment hinders achievement of relevant objectives in science. In the curriculum, there are many words which need to be mastered in order to become literate in the academic discipline of science. A carefully chosen video tape shown to students to introduce a new science unit of study may be used to assist pupils to acquire new concepts and words which may be jotted down. At the end of the presentation, pupils may compare their lists by having the teacher print each on the chalkboard, avoiding duplications. Word and vocabulary study are valuable for their own sake as well as for use in school and in society (Moore and Sampson (2008).

Concepts studied must be shown as being related to each other in ongoing science units of study. For example, in a unit on simple machines, pupils may study a lever, a pulley, an inclined plane, a screw, a wheel and axle, among others. The science teacher must demonstrate the use of each by having real objects such as a lever, an inclined plane, a pulley, and a screw. Pictorial forms of each simple machine need to be discussed in sequence, followed by pupils seeing the related concept for each in print, large enough for all to see clearly. The relationship of words need to be printed in a concept web. Pupils might then refer to the concept web to review, rehearse, and assess previous learnings. It is surprising how many pupils will talk to each other about concepts on the word web as well as those on the word wall. Pupils need to think about and apply what has been acquired in order to have adequate background information and increasingly become scientifically literate (Ediger, 2006).

Classroom Environment

The classroom needs to be conducive to pupil learning. Rudeness, inconsiderateness, and not caring for each other hinders learner progress. Relevant words and concepts need to be studied by pupils with the level of application involved. A variety of interesting, purposeful procedures must be used in engage pupils in achieving objectives in this area.

REFERENCES

Alien, Rick (2008),"Leveraging Technology to Improve Literacy," *Education Update*, 50 (10), 1,3,6.

Ediger, Marlow (2007), "The Substitute Teacher in Reading Instruction," *The SubJournal*, 8 (2), 67-73.

Ediger, Marlow (2007), *School Science Education.* New Delhi, India: Discovery Publishing House.

Ediger, Marlow (2006), "Writing in the Mathematics Curriculum," *Journal of Instructional Psychology*, 33 (2), 120-123.

Moore, Leeann, and Mary Beth Sampson (2008), "Field Based Teacher Preparation: An Organized Analysis of Enabling Conditions," *Education*, 129 (1), 3-16.

National Research Council (1996), *National Science Education Standards*. Washington, DC: The Academy Press.

Reutzel, D. Ray, et. al. (2008), "Scaffolded Silent Reading: A Complement to Guided Repeated Oral Reading That Works!" *The Reading Teacher*, 62 (3), 194-211.

Wessler, Stephen (2008), "Civility Speaks Up," *Educational Leadership*, 66 (1), 44-48.

Zales, Charlotte Ruppe, and Connie S. Unger (2008), "The Science and Literacy Framework," *Science and Children*, 46 (3), 42-45.

23

Oral Communication in Science Lessons and Units of Study

The four language skills—listening, speaking, reading, and writing—interact. Growth in one area of the four interacts and makes for achievement in another. For example, a good listener should achieve more in using what has been learned involving improved speaking. Reading, as well as writing, too, provides excellent content for oral communication. The science teacher may be a positive role model in the classroom in oral communication of which vocabulary development is an important facet of experience. Reddy (2006) listed the following pertaining to vocabulary growth and development in science :

- vocabulary has an important relationship between decoding and comprehension. Vocabulary is perceived as words and meanings in the shared experience of the reader and the author. This relationship increases as reading becomes a primary tool of learning in the middle grades and the high school.
- effective teaching of vocabulary demands that it be an active process that engages students in learning new words in order to build conceptual

representations of vocabulary in multiple contextual situations.

- application of remedial vocabulary instruction requires the linking of instructional strategies to the type of designed learning outcomes and student's learning capabilities.
- vocabulary knowledge supports the reader's processing of text and interacting with the author, which in turn supports the formation and validation of concepts and new learning.
- vocabulary knowledge is an indicator of student's real and vicarious experiences. Children can neither comprehend nor understand what they read unless they have some knowledge of the concepts represented in print. Knowing the meaning of words goes beyond simple definitions and getting the grist from their context. Vocabulary instruction is most effective when it is based on the association of children's experiences and concepts with the words they are learning.
- reader's conceptual and experimental backgrounds are key components in vocabulary development. Background experiences enable readers to develop and refine concepts that words represent.
- vocabulary instruction should include explicit instruction, appropriate practice, and broad based opportunities for language development in a variety of texts.

Content from reading provides subject matter for oral communication activities as in discussions. A variety of rich, developmentally appropriate experiences assists in securing background information in communicating ideas orally, useful in listening, reading and writing. Oral communication has always been a major objective of instruction. The Trivium of the Middle Ages consisted of grammar, rhetoric, and logic.

Rhetoric (public speaking) was combined with grammar and logic to influence others in the societal arena. Cicero, the great Roman orator, placed major emphasis upon public speaking to stress the importance of convincing others to accept selected rules and regulations.

Communicating well with others orally is salient in the science curriculum. Communication, here, involves a sender and one or more receivers. There are a plethora of means in communicating ideas in science such as audio recordings, video tapes, television, CD ROMS, DVDs, non-verbally, films, among others. Orally, with the spoken voice, still is a major way of communication between and among pupils and the teacher. The human voice is flexible device which is a part of the individual and does not necessarily need attending physical equipment. There are many purposes involved in the process of communicating ideas (Ediger, 2008).

Purposes in Communication in Science

Clarity is always important in oral communication since the listener needs to understand what is said. Stress is a significant concept to use in oral communication. Here, the speaker says single words louder or softer within a sentence to amplify intentions in oral communication. If the teacher says,"We will now do a science experiment." the emphasis is upon doing a science experiment rather than a different kind of learning activity or in a different academic discipline. With effective use of stress in teaching and learning situations, the science teacher increases proficiency in teaching. It indicates a lack of monotony in the communication process and the presence of enthusiasm. Selected concepts and generalizations which pupils are to master might well receive adequate stress to indicate what is salient to learn. Heavy stress of spoken words shown in a sentence involve placing an exclamation mark shown at the end of a written sentence (Ediger, 2007).

A second important concept to emphasize in oral communication when teaching science is pitch. Thus, some words are pitched higher than others in context to show the following within the same sentence such as,

- "He did well in conducting the science experiment?" Here, the science teacher pitches the ending words higher to have students comment on the process. It is not stated as a perceived fact. An interrogative sentence is then in evidence.
- "He did well in conducting the science experiment." Here, the teacher orally communicates a fact or opinion with the spoken voice pitched lowest at the end. A period at the end of the written equivalent indicates a fact or opinion was communicated orally.
- "He did well in conducting the science experiment!" An exclamatory sentence shows strong feeling and has an exclamation mark at the end to show this in written work. Each word said orally has a strong stress (National Science Education Standards, 1996).

Thus, meanings change within the same sentence if stress is placed on different words or a word. The same is true of pauses within a sentence. Meanings change depending upon pauses within a sentence. If words in a series, for example, are stated orally, there need to be pauses of adequate length to indicate where commas would appear In writing. Misplaced modifiers, too, cause meanings to change in a sentence :

> He rode to school on a bicycle with a blue scarf. "With a blue scarf," is shown as modifying the bicycle, but it rather should modify the subject of the sentence "He". With a revision, the sentence should read: "With a blue scarf, he rode to school on a bicycle." Misplaced modifiers make for possible distortions in interpretation in oral expressions (Kieffer and Lasaux, 2007).

Reading from a developmentally appropriate basal science textbook or library book orally, involves paying careful attention to punctuation marks. A lack of understanding might well accrue due to omitting or minimizing these punctuation marks. The following lacks clarity if punctuation marks are omitted in a run on sentence: She read from the basal science textbook, wrote a summary, and used a map to show climatic changes in her oral report. To minimize these problems, fluency in oral reading also is aided with assistance in the following :

- difficulties in word recognition. The use of context clues and phonics for initial consonant sounds should help to remedy deficiencies.
- problems in reading in thought units
- practice in oral reading of the selection, prior to its presentation in front of the class
- peers in a group helping each other in these practice sessions (Lockstead, 2008).

Discussions in Science

The writer when supervising university student teachers teach in the public schools has noticed specific kinds of assistance pupils need in order to communicate well in a discussion setting. The following areas need to be strengthened for pupils to communicate well :

- lack of use of complete sentences, such as omitting a subject or a predicate
- minimizing the use of adjectives to modify nouns or adverbs to modify verbs
- use of too few words to express content meaningfully. This may involve the need to clarify content with adjective/adverb phrases and clauses
- rambling on with run on sentences and unnecessary wordage
- not focusing upon the topic being discussed
- use of irrelevant vocabulary terms and ideas (Ediger, 2007).

Discussion should consist of salient learnings which pupils receive from each other. Ideas are changed by an individual as new content is imbibed. Len S.Vygotsky (1978) was a strong advocate of pupils learning in group settings. He believed that ideas "bounce off the minds" of actively involved participants. Higher levels of cognition are then possible. Thus, pupils may discuss solutions to identified problems in an ongoing lesson/unit of study in science. A tentative hypothesis is formed which may be subject to revision within discussion settings. Critical thinking is a part of a discussion whereby facts are separated from opinions, fantasy from reality, and the relevant from the irrelevant. Also, creative thinking is needed to come up with novel, unique ideas for solutions. Creative thinkers are important in the classroom as well as in society. Innovations and improvements come about due to creative ideas expressed in producing goods and services. Thus, science learnings may also be used to write creative poetry, to write and perform plays pertaining to leading scientists, to do drawings in art of volcanic eruptions, among others.

For young children, science picture books may be a good way to introduce and develop ideas pertaining to the natural environment. These may be used by the kindergarten and first grade teachers as well as be used in the home setting. Viewing and discussing igneous, metamorphic, and sedimentary rocks first hand and then looking at their representative illustrations assist pupils to develop interest and understanding in rocks and their uses in society. One may even start with the illustrations and, for example, have pupils look at and discuss simple machines. The writer has noticed in the home setting how young children like and become fascinated with simple machines in pictorial form. Many homes have concrete objects directly related to the illustrations such as a hammer to be used as a lever or a door stop used as a wedge. Also, the writer has noticed how eager young children are in viewing pictures of vertebrates and invertebrates. Vertebrates in pictorial form motivate comments, questions, and problems, even with a short attention span of very young children. Thus, fish, frogs (amphibians), turtles (reptiles), birds, and mammals capture the attention of children. These, among others, provide building blocks for sequential learning in children. Readiness for acquiring more complex facts, concepts, and generalizations are then in the offing.

Interest in science must be developed at a young age with oral communication being inherent in these ongoing learning activities. Visits to museums of natural history and/or viewing visiting displays in a community may well do much to encourage interest in science. Pupils of all ages are excited of and talk among themselves of a dinosaur exhibit. The following display of model dinosaur skeletons was recently observed locally: a brontosaurus, a dipladocus, and a stegosaurs, among others. These provided ideal topics for discussion and elaboration. Many followup activities are then possible including :

- making drawings of these models
- locating more information on dinosaurs
- writing creative stories and poems on dinosaurs
- pantomiming dinosaur life and having others guess which dinosaur is being pantomimed
- doing a booklet on dinosaurs and their environment.

IN CONCLUSION

Pupils need to have a plethora of interesting experiences in an integrated science curriculum. Listening, speaking, reading, and writing activities which accelerate quality science learnings is needed. To develop science literacy, pupils must experience rich opportunities for learning and engagement in the curriculum.

REFERENCES

Ediger, Marlow (2007), *Language Arts Education.* New Delhi, India: Discovery Publishing House.

Ediger, Marlow (2008), "The School and Students in Society," *Journal of Instructional Psychology,* 35 (3), 260-263.

Ediger,Marlow (2007), *School Science Education.* New Delhi, India: Discovery Publishing House.

Kieffer, Michael, and Nancy K, Lesaux (2007), "Breaking Down Words to Build Meaning," *The Reading Teacher,* 61 (2), 146-156.

Lockstead, Larissa (2008), "Scientific Journals: A Creative Assessment Tool," *Science and Children,* 46 (3), 22-26.

National Science Education Standards (1996). Washington, DC: National Research Council, The Academy Press.

Reddy, A. M. (2006), Reading Achievement of High School Pupils in English in Relation to Certain Psycho-Sociological Variables. Tirupati, India: Sri Venkateswara University, pp 16-17. A Ph D thesis evaluated by the writer.

Vygotsky, Len S. (1978), *Mind in Society, the Development of Higher Psychological Processes.* Cambridge, Massachusetts: Harvard University Press.

24

Pupil, Writing and Science Curriculum

Pupils writing across the curriculum is highly significant. The science curriculum can certainly make its many contributions in having learners become effective writers. Being scientifically literate is essential for all in the age of science. Being able to read and write pertaining to information obtained from science lessons and units of study in the school setting is valuable presently as well as in the future. Ideas must be communicated accurately and with precision. Misinformation occurs due to poor quality means of communicating in the written language. Abstract ideas are communicated which the receiver interprets in the concrete.

A developmentally appropriate science curriculum must be emphasized in teaching and learning situations. Otherwise, science learnings may be either too complex whereby frustration occurs or too simple in which boredom may be an end result. The science teacher must adapt different writing strategies to meet pupil needs (Ediger, 2007).

Written Communication in Science

Within each lesson and unit of study, the science teacher must plan quality learning experiences which integrate effectively with experiments, demonstrations, multi-media presentations, as well as reading experiences. Written work by pupils needs to be :

- engaging whereby learners are whole-heartedly involved in communicating ideas
- interesting in terms of experiences provided. Definitely, written work should not "turn" the pupil off in making progress in this area
- involve communicating ideas as accurately and objectively as possible
- meaningfully perceived and communicated so the reader/listener can make the abstract message become concrete
- intrinsically purposeful. Pupils then accept reasons for active participation (Beckstead, 2008).

Engaging pupils in written work in ongoing science lessons and units of study emphasizes that the teacher provide variety in the kinds of activities provided. Among others, the pupil may write up the steps followed in developing a science fair project for exhibit in the local school district annual contest. In the project, the pupil will need to state the purpose for project. Also included are the plans for its development and how the plans were carried out. Hyp.otheses to be tested are written clearly. Self-evaluation by the pupil should be included such as standards listed pertaining to neatness, completeness, and relevance (National National Research Council, 1996).

Interesting writing activities should be provided. Different, rich, and stimulating experiences must be in the offing. These should include journal writing, diary entries, logs, book reports, and summaries. They need to be complete, comprehensive, and indepth. Then too, pupils need encouragement to do voluntary writing. A learning center in the classroom needs to list topics directly related to ongoing science lessons. Pupils might then choose tasks to complete, from among others. Quality written work is to be expected. High expectations for a good product is necessary; however learner success at the same time is salient. Failure in achievement makes for a negative self concept. Too many pupils have feelings of being a failure in written work. This image must be changed to assist each pupil to achieve a healthy and wholesome self concept, and it is possible to improve sequentially to becoming a better writer (Barclay and Schoon, 1999).

Writing as accurately as possible requires a rich vocabulary. Vocabulary growth is a definite part of writing proficiency. When writing, the writer wishes to communicate effectively with others. Variety in vocabulary use is necessary to keep the reader's attention. At the same time, it can be very enjoyable to locate synonyms for a given word to provide for variety in written products. The writer when observing university student teachers teach has noticed frequently that word study need not be boring, but does interest many pupils. Sometimes, brain storming has been used to list as many synonyms as possible for a given word. Pupils then provide as many words as possible for a "match" printed word on the chalkboard. They look at dictionaries, thesauruses, among other sources in book or computer form. When ready, the word processor may be used to communicate ideas for book reports, write-ups of science projects and experiments, summaries, log and diary entries, journal writing, among the many other purposes in writing (Hawkins, 2006).

Since writing is done to communicate with others, it behooves the science teacher to assist pupils to write meaningfully. Sometimes, it is good to have a writer in the classroom share written work with peers to notice the quality of communication involved. Thus, a listener may retell what he/ she comprehended from a written product. Did the writer communicate what was intended? Proper punctuation must be used to notice pauses as well as end of sentences. The science teacher may read aloud to pupils eliminating pauses in order for the listener to notice how meanings change with omitted commas, quotation marks, periods, question marks, and exclamation points. Voice inflection in oral reading also must be noticed by pupils when pitching words higher or lower within a sentence. Also, meanings change of a sentence when specific words are stressed more heavily than others within a sentence. Pitch of words is generally not shown in a written product. Sometimes a writer will underline one or more words in a selection to indicate stress of words, meaning they are said louder than the others.

Meaning may also be indicated in writing by putting in main divisions, as well as subdivisions. As a learning experience, these divisions, in bold print, need to be pointed out by the teacher when pupils read from the basal science textbook. They orient the reader to ensuing subject matter to be read (Ediger, 2007).

Reasons for participating in written work must be stressed prior to learner participation in the writing activity. Thus, if pupils are to write for free and inexpensive science materials, the purpose for writing the letter must be clear to the pupil. Then too if this is an initial learning experience, pupils must know the reasons for writing each part of the business letter such as the heading, inside address, body, closing, and signature. Neatness and clarity are salient criteria to use in appraising the quality of the business letter, written either in long hand or with the use of the word processor. When needed, the science teacher may model these and other learnings in the curriculum. Modelling is a powerful tool to use in teaching science.

Strategies to Use in Teaching and Learning

The science teacher needs to model metacognition approaches of learning in ongoing lessons and units of study. Here, the teacher assists pupil to reflect upon what was learned. Thus after completion of a science experiment, pupils might well be guided to reflect upon the following :

- the sequential steps followed in conducting the experiment
- major concepts and generalizations acquired
- processes followed in discussing the conducting of and the results of the experiment (Ediger, 2006).

Metacognition strategies emphasize thinking about thinking. Thus, the pupil mentally reviews what was learned, what needs more emphasis in learning, and which questions the pupil would like to do research on or discuss more indepth. Encouraging thinking is vital in order that the pupil thinks critically and creatively. Optimal achievement in science is a must!

Inductive learning also must receive its fair share of time in science lessons and units of study. To learn inductively, a pupil is not provided with a lecture or lengthy explanation of subject matter content in a lesson, but rather questions are raised to help the learner find needed answers. A high school physics teacher at a National Science Teacher's Association convention stated that he never answered a pupil's questions with facts, but rather asked another question which assisted the pupil in finding necessary information.

IN CLOSING

Pupils need a variety of rich experiences in writing. They must experience purpose, interest, and meaning in all written work. Writing skills are salient in science but also in the societal arena. The science teacher must integrate written work along with reading, listening, and speaking goals in ongoing lessons and units of study.

REFERENCES

Barclay, D. C., and S. Schoon (1999), "Making the Connection! Science and Literacy," *Childhood Education*, 75 (3),146-152.

Beckstead, Larissa (2008), "Scientific Journals: A Creative Assessment Tool," *Science and Children*, 46 (3), 22-26.

Ediger, Marlow (2007), *Language Arts Education*. New Delhi, India: Discovery Publishing House.

Ediger, Marlow (2007), "Meaning in Reading Instruction", *Reading Improvement*, 44 (4),217-220.

Ediger, Marlow (2006), "Writing in the Mathematics Curriculum", *Journal of Instructional Psychology*, 33 (1), 120-123.

Hawkins, Joanna (2006), "Think Before You Write," *Educational Leadership*, 64 (2), 63-67.

National Research Council (1996), *National Science Education Standards*. Washington, DC: Academy Press.

25

Integrated Science Curriculum

Pupils need to perceive that subject-matter is related in different curriculum areas. It becomes easier to retain learnings if content is sensed as being related. One idea then makes it less complex to relate to others. The degree to which content should be related becomes an issue. How much of subject matter integration should then be emphasized in teaching and learning situations? This might be shown on a continuum, all the way from very minimal to much integration of subject matter taught. A strong consideration here pertains to which science unit of study is being emphasized and how much of meaningful relationships can be shown with other academic disciplines..

Science and the Integration of Subject-matter

Science has its own unique facts, concepts, and generalizations which pupils need to acquire from the earth sciences, the physical sciences, and the biological sciences. Relevant objectives then need to be determined which learners need to attain. The objectives need to be challenging and attainable. Objectives which are too difficult to achieve make for feelings of frustration whereas those being too easy might well make for boredom. Then too, there needs to be a balance among knowledge, skills, and attitudinal ends. Learner achievement needs to be evaluated during the time a unit is taught as well as at the end of the unit. A variety of appraisal techniques must be used in the evaluation process such as :

- teacher daily observation and appraised in terms of quality criteria
- pupil self-evaluation, reflection, and metacognition
- valid and reliable multiple choice and essay test items, teacher developed or mandated tests
- assessment of science projects developed
- evaluation of critical and creative thinking as well as problem solving skills
- appraisal of listening, speaking, reading, and writing skills in science (National Science Education Standards, 1996).

With integration of subject-matter, the science teacher needs to decide at which point this should occur. The integration must be seamless and add value to what is being studied. Thus, integration is not done for the sake of doing so, but rather to project meaning in achieving relevant objectives. For example, in a science unit on "The Changing of the Earth's Surface," pupils may study the causes of tornados in sequential detail. Indepth analysis of tornados is necessary to truly understand selected causes. They might result in serious property damage and loss of life as well as injuries to human beings. The city of Greensburgh, Kansas was almost destroyed completely in a May, 2007 destructive tornado. Related social studies content may include a variety of learning activities pertaining to the deceased and caring for injured people and rebuilding of the city, which is still ongoing. Mathematics understandings include the costs involved monetarily. Psychology might stress the fear, anxieties, and pain, experienced by the inhabitants of

Greensburgh. The integrated science curriculum has numerous advantages :

- it assists pupils to extend knowledge beyond the study of a single academic discipline. However, a pupil should always gain adequate knowledge of what science is and its methods used, to acquire information
- it helps pupils to related science to other academic disciplines. The transfer of knowledge and its use from discipline to discipline might guide pupils to achieve more optimally. Pupils should, however, perceive the content and processes of science pertaining to one academic discipline.
- it promotes pupil learning across the curriculum such as in reading subject matter. Science concepts and generalizations and their meanings are unique to one academic discipline as are those of each of the other academic disciplines
- it has specific kinds of learning activities such as doing experiments which is the heart of the science curriculum; others cut across several academic disciplines such as inquiry learning, problem solving, project methods, critical and creative thinking, as well as cooperative learning.
- it stresses evaluation in terms of teacher observation to notice achievement such as in experimentation, as a learning activity, which requires clarity of criteria to assess the quality of problem identified, the hypotheses developed, and the testing of each tentative hypothesis (Ediger, 2007).

Separate Subjects Discipline and Committee Endeavors

When supervising university student teachers in the public schools, the writer observed the teaching of a sixth grade science unit on invertebrates. The student teacher and the cooperating teacher adhered to teaching specific facts, concepts, and generalizations pertaining to science as a separate academic discipline. Very little attention was given to integrating subject matter from other academic disciplines. Pupils then divided into committees to work on a report of their chosen topic from a list developed by the student teacher and the cooperating teacher. Each committee could then select which classification of invertebrates they wished to work from in gathering necessary information.

The following were listed and both teachers stressed background information on each during the large group sessions :

- the ameba, the paramecium, and the euglena (protozoans)
- sponges (porifera)
- hydras, jellyfish, coral, and sea anemones (coelenterates)
- flatworms such as planarians, flukes, and tapeworms (platyhelminthes)
- segmented worms like earthworms and sandworms (annelida)
- starfish, sea urchin, sea cucumber, and sand dollar (echinodermata)
- clams, scallops, mussels, oysters, slugs, and snails (mollusca)
- shrimp, lobster, crayfish, and crabs (arthropods) (Blough and Schwartz, 1984).

Criteria for working on each committee were discussed and standards for presenting the oral reports were also given. A variety of reference sources were used to gather needed information. One committee chose "shrimp and lobster" for their oral reports. The details of each were developed indepth. In addition to reporting on these two invertebrates, knowledge from other disciplines were integrated into the oral report such as :

- seafood served in restaurants which include shrimp and lobster
- large scale fishing for shrimp and lobster, as a means of earning a living
- raising these invertebrates in farm operations
- characteristics making for the classification of "arthropods."

A second committee chose "earthworms" for their investigation. They described the classification of invertebrates such as "annelids" indepth. In addition to the scientific classification, The committee also integrated the following from other academic subject-matter areas :

- earthworms being a part of compost piles
- their role in maintaining fertile soils
- earthworms eaten as food in certain nations
- characteristics of invertebrates known as "annelida".

For example, in each of the social science disciplines, invertebrates may be studied from their separate subject area:

- economics as in ways of earning a livelihood such as fishing for oysters
- regions in geography where specific invertebrates are located
- history in the study of rare species and those no longer in existence
- sociology and the indepth knowledge of culture involving exotic foods such as chocolate covered, fried grasshoppers
- political science with its rules and regulations on fishing for shrimp and lobster.

There are selected criteria which need to be followed in developing an integrated science curriculum. Science content must be at the center of the planning. The principles of science must not be overshadowed by content from other academic disciplines. The latter must enhance the planned science unit of study. Objectives for pupil attainment need to be carefully chosen in terms of being relevant and useful in school and in society. They must be ordered or sequenced to optimize learner achievement and progress. Learning activities should be aligned with the stated objectives. They need to be interesting, meaningful, and possess purpose. Appraisal procedures need to be varied to take into account the assessment of experimentation. It is difficult for paper/pencil tests to measure achievement adequately in this salient facet of learning. Teacher observation in terms of important criteria must be used here. Otherwise, multiple choice and essay tests may be used to measure acquired facts, concepts, and generalizations in science. Tests must be valid and reliable (National Research Council, 2000).

Pertaining to the integration and relationship of different academic disciplines, Jackson *et al.*, 2008) wrote the following:

> Making connections is always an important task for teachers. Science teachers are encouraged to connect new lear-nings with student's prior knowledge, learning with student interests, learning with cultural experiences, and classroom activities across academic disciplines. Strategies that facilitate these connections help teachers enrich and enhance instruction.

REFERENCES

Blough, Glenn, and Schwartz, Julius (1984), Elementary School Science and How to Teach It. New York: CBS Publishing Company.

Ediger, Marlow (2007), *School Science Education.* New Delhi, India: Discovery Publishing House.

Jackson, Julie, *et al.* (2008), "Connections, charts, and BookTAlks," *Science and Children*, 46 (3), 27-31.

National Research Council (2000), *How People Learn.* Washington, DC: National Academy Press.

National Science Education Standards (1996), National Research Council. Washington, DC: The Academy Press.

26

Children's Literature and Science Curriculum

A quality children's literature programme needs to be correlated with ongoing science lessons and units of study. It can enhance and enrich the science curriculum. Pupils tend to enjoy reading library books and the the literature may assist pupils to explore topics in greater depth. In addition to science experiments, demonstrations, and multi-media, children's literature is another avenue of learning science concepts and generalizations. Voluntarily, pupils may pursue personal interests and purposes in science (Ediger and Rao, 2005).

Children's Literature and Science

An attractive bulletin board display showing selected book jackets of new library books should be readily visible to children in the classroom. The science teacher needs to refer to the bulletin board while introducing library books to the class. This provides readiness for choosing a library book to read. Subject-matter presented provides background information for reading. Pupils then have an overview of content in a library book, making it easier to comprehend.

During spare time in the school day, pupils may read science content. While supervising university student teachers in the public schools, the writer experienced the use of library book content in a science lesson discussion. Thus instead of using the basal text, pupils presented ideas on "The Changing Surface of the Earth" from related library book content. The discussion was engaging and lively with comments from almost each pupil. Smaller groups make it possible for more frequency of participation by each child and this was observed in a different observational visit. A good library of science books is a must! It is a way of further securing pupil interest in different topics in science (Ediger, 2007-08).

There are more approaches in stressing children's literature in science. During story time, the teacher needs to read aloud to pupils carefully chosen library books on science content. He/she needs to read with voice inflection, appropriate pitch, and enunciation. Obtaining and maintaining learner attention is important. If children are of primary school age, it is good to show the related illustrations as content is being read orally. This assists these young children to understand subject matter read. The speed of oral reading needs to engage good listening. Periodically, the teacher needs to ask interesting questions pertaining to content read. These questions and forthcoming answers might well propel pupils to acquire further information on their own (Ray, 2006).

The content read aloud may motivate pupils to select a problem area to solve. The problem takes time to solve and involves deliberation and time to secure necessary information. The library books, science experiments, and the internet, among other reference sources, may be used. Critical thinking needs to be emphasized in separating facts from opinions, fantasy from reality, and accurate from inaccurate content. Objective information then needs to be secured. Individual or small group endeavors may be involved in problem solving. Creative thinking, too, may be stressed in coming up with new solutions to problems. Creative thinking also needs to be encouraged because improvements in school and in society come about due to novel, unique ideas developed. Thus, library books read to children do help learners to branch out in their thinking (National Research Council, 1996).

As another science library book activity, a certain period of time needs to be set aside during the school day for pupils to read a self selected library book. Generally, a pupil will choose a book of personal interest and on his/her reading level. Pupils tend to select sequential library books which are meaningful and they perceive purpose in their reading. Individualized reading motivates learners to read since they have personal ownership due self selection of reading materials. Developing a life long interest in reading and learning about science is salient (American Association for the Advancement of Science, 1993).

When peers read a science library book together and share its contents, they may well engage in higher levels of cognition since ideas circulate among participants. Vygotsky (1978) advocated a social situation in learning whereby ideas "bounce off the minds of participants" and are scaffolded. Scaffolding occurs when content is too difficult to understand but is achievable with smaller sequential steps of learning. The sequential steps of learning are based upon the pupil's previous knowledge and lead to the initial complex idea. Science teachers, too, may use scaffolding in teaching by identifying an idea not understood but achievable through smaller ordered learning activities. These order steps of learning are based upon what pupils do understood, leading to the more complicated learning. When pupils in a committee setting see illustrations in a library book, they decide what they already know about the topic. It assists pupils to integrate and use previous knowledge to predict what will transpire. Also, pupils raise questions for which they may read the ensuing library book to secure answers. These experiences aid in comprehending more fully of what will be read (Luchmann, 2007).

Extending learnings here might involve doing a project for a science fair or for an ongoing science unit of study. The writer has served as a judge at numerous science fairs and feels positive about many projects appraised. The projects are an outgrowth of the science curriculum, student independent reading, interests, and thought. Along with the quality of the project, the writer looked for and evaluated the following :

- where the idea came from for the construction of the project. It is good if the ideas come from the learner, meaning it is not dictated by parents or the teacher. However, support by both is important
- the care with which sequential steps in planning the project were stressed
- the purpose of the project
- the hypotheses to be tested in the project
- sources of information used.

A few of the projects evaluated included solar panels, a model of the solar system, control of wind and water erosion of soil, a model earthquake structure, a system of wind energy, and a model flood control project (Bowers, 2005).

Communicating with Parents

In a quality science programme of instruction, it is good to develop and maintain open lines of communication with parents. The children's literature programme is no exception. The school reading program needs to be connected with that of the home. E-mail, face to face meetings, and the voice recorder may be used as media for the messages. Both science teacher and parents need to exchange messages pertaining to :

- pupil interest and general progress made in reading
- pupil achievement in comprehension, including higher levels of cognitio
- pupil mastery of word recognition skills

- pupil problems in reading fluently
- pupil skills in working with others in cooperative learning (Ediger, 2008).

Personal achievement is important for each pupil. Pupils individually must learn to monitor their very own progress. This means that the child is not a word caller, but checks the self to ascertain personal comprehension as the act of reading continues. Thus, the learner can then say aloud and attach meaning to content read. Comprehension is the objective in reading science subject matter (Hansen, 2003).

REFERENCES

American Association for the Advancement of Science (1993), *Benchmarks for Science Literacy.* New York: Oxford University Press.

Bowers, Susan (2005), "The Portfolio Process: Questions for Implementation and Practice," *The College Student Journal*, 39 (4), 754-758.

Ediger, Marlow, and D. Bhaskara Rao (2005), Teaching Science in *Elementary Schools.* New Delhi, India: Discovery Publishing House.

Ediger, Marlow (2007), "Psychology of Parental Invovlement in Reading," *Reading Improvement*, 45 (1), 46-52.

Ediger, Marlow (2008), "Student Vocabulary Development in the Science Curriculum," *Connecticut Journal of Science Education*, 45 (1), 12-13.

Luchmann, A. L. (2007), "Identity Development as a Lens to Science Teacher Preparation, *Science Education*, 91, 822-839,

Hansen, Laurie (2003), "Science in any Language," *Science and Children*, 41 (3), 35-39.

National Research Council (1995), *National Science Education Standards*, Washington DC: National Academy Press.

Ray, Katie Wood (2006), "What Are You Thinking?" *Educational Leadership*, 64 (2), 58-62.

Vygotsky, L. S. (1978), *Mind in Society: the Development of Higher Psychological Processes.* Cambridge, Massachusetts: Harvard University Press.

27

Reading Comprehension in Science Curriculum

Students may experience difficulty in reading science subject-matter. It is very important that each comprehends well when reading content in science as well as understanding these ideas indepth. The teacher needs to help each student in comprehending when being engaged in reading to secure facts, concepts, and generalizations in science (Cuniff and McMillen 1996). What might be done to assist learners in achieving when reading?

Increasing Reading Comprehension in Science

Reading may be done to secure background information in attaching meaning to a science experiment. Readiness in benefiting from the experiment is a must. Necessary background knowledge for reading then needs to be activated in in order to understand subject-matter in the ongoing activity.

Reading may also be done to substantiate, modify, or refute student conclusions realized from the science experiment. It might be necessary to redo the experiment and/or view other reference sources to test the outcomes of the initial science experiment. In supervising university student teachers in the public schools, the writer observed a student teacher and the cooperating teacher viewing and discussing related illustrations from a basal science textbook. Much interest was developed to pursue the reading experience. New words which appeared in the scripted materials were printed on a flipchart. In this way, students could see and take careful notice during the discussion of each as they were used in the textbook. Questions pertaining to the textbook illustrations were identified and printed on the chalkboard. They were referred to in the reading activity. These experiences provided readiness for reading science subject matter and all were related to the science experiment discussed above (Ediger, 2007).

If the students in the class are homogeneously grouped and are good readers, the illustrations, alone, may be discussed to motivate the class in the reading activity. Otherwise, fluency in reading should also occur. Reading hesitantly and haltingly hinders comprehension in reading experiences. Readiness experiences assist in avoiding these situations.

There are a plethora of followup activities in reading and might well include the following :

- check the conclusions with that of the science experiment
- develop a related science experiment
- write up the conclusions within a committee and file for future reference
- do a diorama, write poetry, and/or make a drawing of the completed science experiment
- in a peer setting, identify a project to complete and/ or
- make a model, related to the experiment
- put new science words encountered on the science wall
- develop a bulletin board display (Ediger, 2008).

Strategies to Stress in Teaching

The difficulties in reading to understand science subject-matter may be minimized with foresight and skilful methods used in teaching. A university student teacher (ST) supervised by the writer in the public schools used an opaque projector to enlarge the print contained in the basal textbook so all could see the content clearly in a small group of five struggling readers. She discussed the related illustrations to develop background information for the reading activity. The purpose also was stated for reading the science subject-matter. The science teacher read the content aloud while pointing to each word/phrase. Students were carefully observed and assisted to follow the script carefully while the subject matter was read orally. The second reading followed with the teacher and students reading aloud together as the former still pointed to each word being read. Then students in the small group read the content collectively without teacher help. The latter still pointed to each word being read. Students generally were able to read the selection independently. In this way, students developed a basic science vocabulary and comprehended subject matter read. Later, these students participated with the others in discussing vital science concepts and generalizations, such as motion, matter, friction, and force. By using this procedure, struggling readers may :

- read the same ideas as others in the classroom
- read fluently without stumbling on unknown words
- read science subject matter, concentrating on comprehension
- read in gaining a basic sight vocabulary through rereading science subject matter in a non-threatening manner (Gill, 2008).

In all procedures of science reading instruction, students need to monitor, individually, their very own comprehension of subject matter. By monitoring what has been read, students may reflect upon comprehended facts, concepts, and generalizations and not merely pronouncing words while reading. Metacognition strategies, also, are important. Here, students are taught to think about thinking. Thus, the student thinks, for example, about the central idea of all the inherent ideas acquired. Parts are then synthesized into a complex whole. Metacognition may also be emphasized in rehearsing what has been learned to notice gaps in knowledge and skills. Thus, there may be gaps in the past problem or project completed with involved knowledge and skills. Gaps can be ameliorated through a process known as scaffolding. Here, the science teacher notices where a student is in achievement presently and compares it with a developmentally more complex ideal. This gap may be minimized with a set of carefully planned, sequential learning experiences (Ediger, 2007).

IN CONCLUSION

To show excellence in comprehending science subject matter. Students need assistance to develop background information pertaining to what will be read, thus connecting what is known with what will be read. It is also good to have students relate the content to their very own personal lives in terms of uses to be made of the information. Vocabulary development is an inherent part of becoming a good reader in science. The reading activities need to center around the heart of science which is quality experimentation. Learnings acquired need to be extended to emphasize indepth understanding of vital facts, concepts, and generalizations. Recreational reading, too, needs to be stressed in which accurate science content may be read. The teacher needs to be aware of library books which are available in this area which might interest and challenge learner curiosities (National Research Center, 1996).

Important trends need to be studied by teachers, including how technology and computers may assist students to achieve complex, but achievable objectives. There needs to be high teacher expectations for each student's achievement! (Horejsi, 2003).

REFERENCES

Cuniff, Patricia A., and Janet K. McMillen (1996), "Field Studies," *The Science Teacher*, 63, 51-55.

Ediger, Marlow (2007), *Science Curriculum and Instruction*. New Delhi, India: Discovery Publishing House.

Ediger, Marlow (2007), "Meaning in Reading Instruction," *Reading Improvement*, 44 (4), 217-220.

Ediger, Marlow (2008), "Leadership in the School Setting," *Education*, 129(1), 17-20.

Gill, Sharon Ruth (2008), "The Comprehension Matrix: A Tool for Designing Comprehension Strategies, *The Reading Teacher*, 62(2), 106-115.

Horejsi, Martin (2003), "Making Technolgy Inclusive," *Science and Children*, 41 (3), 20-24.

National Science Education Standards. Washington, DC: the National Academy Press.

28

Pre-student Teaching Field Experiences

Prior to student teaching, pre-service teachers need to engage in early field experiences. The early field experience may be taken simultaneously with methods of teaching classes along other university professional education requirements. These experiences need to provide readiness activities for student teaching. Also, the early field experience assists the student to integrate what has been acquired from general education, and educational psychology/ sociology course work. The student needs to be able to incorporate, relate, and integrate previously acquired learnings. The ultimate goal is to develop a professional teacher for the public schools.

Early Field Experiences

Early field activities should model what a regular, licensed teacher experiences, but on an earlier level of achievement. What should this model consist of and how will it provide readiness for student teaching? These early experiences must be sequential for the student so that success is experienced. A good self-concept for teaching and learning is important.

Professional cooperating teachers need to be available to supervise the pre-service activities. They provide a model to emulate and can offer suggestions for improving these early field experiences.

A variety of positive teaching models should be be experienced. They reveal diverse philosophies of teaching and learning. Future teachers may then be able to better adapt instruction to public school pupils when being fully licensed. Models shown in teaching may represent :

- inductive and deductive procedures of instruction
- problem solving and projects methods
- small group work and individualized approaches
- multi-media and computer activities
- concrete, semi-concrete, and abstract learning activities
- recreational reading such as sustained silent reading (SSR)
- use of basals, library books, and other reference sources (Ediger, 2008).

Pre-student experiences should also include specific examples of good teaching. The rational should be given by the teacher for using each method of teaching. Thus, if a basal reader is used in teaching pupils, the university student needs to observe the sequence of steps followed in providing readiness for reading :

- viewing illustrations pertaining to the ensuing story to be read. This activity provides background information to the pupil to comprehend contents
- pupil prediction as to what the story will be about. Later, after reading the contents, the pupil may check his/her prediction(s)
- observing the new words, to be met in print, printed on the white board or presented by the computer on an enlarged screen

- discussing the contextual meaning of each new word
- assisting pupils with unidentified words during the reading activity
- interacting with the content after its reading with a discussion, as well as critical and creative thinking experiences (Ediger, 2007).

Additional follow-up activities may include creatively dramatizing the story contents, drawing a related picture of a concept or generalization, and/or making a model.

The student may then either teach a supervised reading lesson or assist in its presentation. He/she may also observe and assist in teaching the other curriculum areas such as in :

- a developmental appropriate lesson in mathematics (e.g. borrowing in subtraction)
- a power point presentation to initiate a new social studies unit
- an experiment performed as an integral part of an ongoing science lesson (Kucan, 2007).

The university student needs to have ample opportunities to discuss and evaluate each of the above named lessons. Metacognition is an important concept pertaining to teaching which may be brought in during the discussion and assessment. Metacognition emphasizes thinking about thinking. Here, the teacher and the university student think about what transpired sequentially in a completed lesson taught. The following questions and possible answers may be pondered :

- were pupils attentive during the lesson?
- how might inattentive pupils be encouraged to become interested in the ongoing lesson?
- did pupils perceive purpose or reasons for learning?
- were individual differences provided for?
- what might be improved upon in implementing the lesson? (Gardner, 1993).

By thinking about the lesson implementation and its results, the university student and the teacher may assist the former in evaluating to provide feedback for future lessons to be taught. The university student in pre-student teaching field experiences needs to incorporate a repertoire of quality teaching experience through observation and providing assistance to the regular classroom teacher. Active involvement in teaching is to be encouraged. Gradually and subsequently, the pre-student teacher assimilates and uses diverse psychologies and philosophies of teaching. The university student needs to diagnose learning situations and work toward remediation of what hinders pupils in learning. Each pupil needs to attain as optimally as possible. Diagnosis in reading, as an example, may pertain to the following specific problems :

- not using phonics when appropriate. In reading situations where there is consistency between grapheme and phoneme, the learner needs to be aided in identifying a word correctly.
- incorrectly using context clues with wild attempts made at determining the unknown word.
- not paying attention to punctuation marks.
- incorrect phrasing of words. Thus, the learner fails to read in thought units.
- improper use of stress, pitch, and enunciation while reading aloud.
- not monitoring his/her own thinking by engaging in word calling.

The teacher must assist pupils in practicing what needs to be remedied when reading. With effective instruction, many pupil weaknesses may be minimized or eliminated (Ediger and Rao, 2007).

Improving Observations

Pre-Student teachers in field experiences will do considerable observing of actual classroom and school situations. Assistance must be given as to guidelines to use in the observational setting. These may well include the following :

- view any teaching and learning situation in terms of how it benefits each learner. How might pupils be assisted who are not actively engaged in learning?
- what specifically might a pupil need assistance in who appears to lack motivation in learning?
- which materials of instruction might be of benefit to motivate learners?
- what might the teacher do to help pupils who truly have major deficits in achievement?
- which kinds of experiences aid pupils in progressing toward goal attainment?
- which criteria should be used in grouping pupils for instruction?
- how might a community be organized to truly assist pupils in reading progress, or other curriculum area?
- what kinds of inservice education programs will assist teachers to improve in the instructional arenas? (Monke, 2006).

Pre-student teachers should meet together periodically to discuss and analyze problems pertaining to the above areas. Hopefully much thought will go into improving the pre-student teacher field experiences. Specific recommendations and thought will aid university student teachers in continual development to become good student teachers and then progress to being quality professional teachers.

Evaluation of Pupil Progress

Pre-student teachers need to develop a philosophy of teaching and learning. Objectives for pupils to achieve need to be open-ended. It should not be based on achieving factual knowledge, largely or only, where its an either or situation in being successful learners in goal attainment. Rather, knowledge and skills are subject to modification and change. Pupil self evaluation is important. There is subjectivity in the evaluation process. Knowledge and skills are learned to be used and not for their sake. It is the pupil who sequences knowledge and skills. The teacher provides leadership and guidance to assist learners to use learnings in school and in society.

REFERENCES

Ediger, Marlow (2008), "Leadership in the School Setting," *Education*, 129(1), 17-20.

Ediger, Marlow (2007), "Meaning in Reading Instruction," *Reading Improvement*, 44 (4), 217-220.

Ediger, Marlow, and D. Bhaskara Rao (2007), *Reading Curriculum and Instruction.* New Delhi, India: Discovery Publishing House.

Gardner, Howard (1993), *Multiple Intelligences: Theory Into Practice*, New York: Basic Books.

Kucan, Linda 2007), "Insights from Teachers Who Analyzed Transcripts of Their Own Classroom Discussions," *The Reading Teacher*, 63 (3), 228-236).

Monke, Lowell (2006), "The Overdominace of Computers," *Educational Leadership*, 63 (4), 20-23.

29

Science Fairs and Student

Developing a project for a science fair can be highly interesting as well as purposeful for the learner. When supervising university student teachers in the public schools, the writer has noticed much enthusiasm shown by students in doing individual and committee projects in science. Sometimes, these projects have been shown at a local science fair in the school district. This makes it possible for all students to participate. It should be voluntary, not a requirement, to participate. Some students do need encouragement to complete a science project and complete it in time for showing. People at these science fairs tend to ask a plethora of questions pertaining to these projects, making it necessary for learners to be well prepared to provide quality answers as well as secure additional information for further indepth study (Ediger, 1996).

Criteria for Project Development

There are salient factors for students to consider when developing a project, generally from an ongoing science unit of study. Thus, students should perceive a purpose. The purpose should ideally come from the student. Having parental involvement is good since this may well serve as a motivator, but the purpose as well as planning and carrying out the plans should be the role of the student. Purposes should be discussed indepth with the science teacher. Relevancy must be considered in thinking about a purpose for project development. Thus, the science fair project must be perceived as being salient. Which purposes may be considered important when developing a science fair project, pertaining to an ongoing unit of study, "The Changing and Sustainable Surface of the Earth?"

- making a model volcano from plaster of paster and using tempera paint to outline specific features. Models may also be made of mudslides, watersheds, soil erosion, flood waters to contain flood waters, among others
- developing a model scene to prevent soil erosion with terraces, trees, strip cropping, and grass
- doing a model solar unit together with a listing and illustrations of pollution in its diverse forms from different energy sources
- making a detailed set of drawings on clean, renewable sources of energy such as wind power, solar panels on homes, geothermal, as well as other sustainable and clean sources of energy (Ediger, 2000).

Projects developed need to possess quality standards of accuracy, neatness, and thoroughness. Each project must posses related statements on the purpose of the project, the involved planning, the carrying out of the plans, and how each was evaluated with the accompanying desired criteria.

Each project needs to be developmentally appropriate for the involved student. Projects may be developed individually or within a committee of learners. Gathering and appraising relevant information from a variety of reference sources is vital to the project being developed. The student needs to be highly knowledgeable of his/her project. Those observing the projects at the science fair, no doubt, will tend to ask many related questions and the developer needs to be ready to answer questions proficiently. As a judge at many school science fairs, the writer asked the developers of each item judged, the following questions, as an example :

- where did you get the ideas from in developing your project?
- did you work individually on this project or were others involved?
- which reference sources and what information did you use to complete your project?
- how would you judge the quality of your project? Why do you think so?
- what, if anything, would you do differently next time? (National Research Council, 1996).

Pictures taken of student projects may become excellent parts of a portfolio for the evaluation of learner progress as well as for newspaper write-ups of science fair entries. Pertaining to the use of digital cameras, Supon (2006) wrote the following positive uses :

> Digital camera use increases analytical skills and can be used as a means of assessing student performance. Having students know what high quality is can effectively be documented through photographs. When students recognize similarities and differences of their performance through photos, students become reflective and effective with self assessment. This process increases better performance, performance.

It is recognized that digital cameras have a definite impact in today's classroom. With effective usage, multidimensional learning opportunities occur for students.

(John) Dewey's point abut the destructive power of schools should make us ask ourselves some fundamental questions. What is the purpose of school? What dispositions about learning, reading, school, the world, and the self do we want to cultivate? Ask young children why they go to school. You will hear nothing about joy (Wolk, 2008). Wolk goes on to analyze the concept of joy in school for students :

- Find the pleasure in learning
- Give students choice
- Let students create things
- Show off student work
- Take time to tinker
- Make school space inviting
- Get outside (the classroom)
- Read good books
- Transform assessment.

Too frequently, students find learning as being drudgery as well as being boring. Science fairs might well replace these feelings with doing things which bring satisfaction and self esteem. Students own the project being contemplated and completed. By providing opportunities for decision making, learners are engaged in doing what is salient presently in school as well as throughout life in society. The choice might well stressing creative endeavors. Novelty and uniqueness are inherent. There are times, too, for students to share what has been completed with others. Here, the student may explain and answer questions of the questioner. Critical thinking may be a part of the learnings experienced in securing information related directly to queries. By providing time for project development, students experiment with new procedures and approaches. A variety of materials need to be available in the classroom to reward creative work of learners working on science projects. Excursions might also be necessary to motivate students to identify possible concepts for project work. Traditional methods of learning should not be minimized such as reading experiences to obtain ideas for science fair projects. Library books as well as the basal science textbook may be used as reference sources (Zales and Unger, 2008). Innovative methods of evaluation might well include use of portfolios to show student progress. Within the portfolio, representative student work in science needs to be incorporated such as :

- written science book reports revealing salient concepts and generalizations secured
- digital camera photos of science experiments and science projects developed
- science journals and diaries kept on classroom science lessons and units of study experienced
- field trips and excursions made, directly related and integral to subject matter studied.

The portfolio may be bound and shown as a science fair project. It must be appealing and gain parental and audience attention! Criteria for its development and assessment need to be in the offing. Transforming assessment, from testing to innovative approaches, is important (Ediger, 2006).

REFERENCES

Ediger, Marlow (1996), "Evaluation of Pupil Achievement, *Education Magazine*, 45-53.

Ediger, Marlow (2000), "The Role of the Principal in the Science Curriculum," *Experiments in Education*, 28 (2), 23-29.

Ediger, Marlow (2006), "Testing vs Portfolios to Assess Achievement," *OASCD Journal.*

National Research Council (1996), *National Science Education Standards*. Washington, DC: National Academy Press.

Supon, Viola (2006), "Using Digital Cameras for Multidimensional Learning in K-12 Classrooms", *Journal of Instructional Psychology,* 33 (2), 154-156.

Wolk, Steven (2008), "Joy in School", *Educational Leadership,* 66 (1), 8-13.

Zales, Charlotte Rappe, and Connie S. Unger (2008), "The Science and Literacy Framework", *Science and Children*, 46 (3), 42-45.

30

Leadership to Improve Science Curriculum

The science curriculum needs to be studied and updated periodically. The best objectives, learning activities, and appraisal procedures need to be implemented. Each of us lives in a scientific world. The knowledge explosion in science has been here for some time. New medical practices to improve and prolong life, better means of producing goods and services, as well as innovative means of transportation and communication, among others, have helped to make for a more meaningful and quality life style.

There also are hindrances to an improved society such as wars which kill and maim military personnel as well as civilians, destroy buildings, pollute, and make for hatred toward others. These, among other problems, need identification and solutions made.

To have appropriate and needed innovations in the science curriculum, leadership is necessary. Within a public school setting, there are individuals and groups which may provide the needed leadership. One person may be designated to carry on the role of being a leader to improve the science curriculum, namely the school principal. However, each teacher might also be a leader in working toward a quality science curriculum (Ediger, 2007).

Efforts Toward Improving the Science Curriculum

Grade level meetings are one method to use in science curriculum improvement. Thus, within the building, fourth grade teachers, as an example, may meet together in a planned series of meetings. If the school has only two teachers per grade level, combining fourth, fifth, and sixth grade science teachers is a good possibility. As one task of the group, objectives may be discussed and be more specific as compared those on mandated tests. Meaningful, agreed upon objectives for student achievement is important. Vague, hazy objectives may not be of much assistance to the science teacher. By discussing objectives, the involved teachers may also notice omitted relevant objectives such as critical and creative thinking, as well as problem solving. Attitudinal objectives, also, may be slighted unless emphasized in teaching (Ediger, 2008).

Along with discussing objectives, these science teachers may also assess the learning activities to achieve each objective. Here, teachers learn about different possibilities to assist learners to achieve, grow, and develop. Too frequently, teachers have used the same kinds of activities which have not motivated students. Perhaps, too much stress has been placed upon reading about science rather than doing science experiments and demonstrations. There needs to be rational balance among diverse kinds of learning experiences such as concrete, semi-concrete, and abstract activities (Ediger, 2007-2008). In addition to experimentation and reading, the following also need to be considered as possibilities to provide for individual differences :

- whole class and peer discussion groups
- construction activities such as making a solar collector in an ongoing unit of study
- art work such as developing a science mural illustrating a concept and/or generalization

- poetry writing directly related to an ongoing lesson
- reading and reporting on a library book involving a specific topic in science
- debates such as advocating a specific for of energy such as wind, water, solar, nuclear, coal, geothermal, among others
- dramatic activities including the life of a famous scientist
- individualized reading on a self chosen science library book (Hansen, 2003).

The teachers in the inservice education experience need to view valid and reliable evaluation techniques to appraise progress which may well include :

- student and teacher self evaluation in terms of desired criteria
- teacher observation, using recommended standards, to assess and diagnose/remediate
- teacher written tests such as essay and multiple choice test items.

Grade level meetings should aid to improve the science curriculum. Teacher feedback to the group of what seemingly was successful in the classroom from the involved discussions needs to be analyzed and reported upon (Ediger, 2008).

Faculty meetings may also be devoted to improving science teaching. Problems in teaching science need to be discussed. Ideas presented must be respected and flow freely among participants. Ideas for discussion involving improving the science curriculum may come from any faculty member. An agenda committee should prioritize the problems identified for discussion, if many suggestions are made. The best ideas for teaching science should result from the faculty meeting. A faculty member may volunteer to try out ah innovative idea in the classroom and report back to the group. Then too, committees may be formed in volunteering to work on a problem area. Among others, these may include the following :

- using inductive teaching
- having students engage in problem solving which includes having a tentative solution to the problem in hypothesis form, and then testing the hypothesis
- developing an integrated science/social studies unit on alternative sources of energy
- stressing quality sequence in science
- using writing activities in ongoing lessons and units of study (Ohanian and Kovacs, 2007).

An additional approach at inservice education is the workshop concept. Faculty members need to be surveyed to ascertain which facets of science instruction need the most emphasis. Items in the survey need to be clearly stated with participants indicating their first, second, and third choices to be covered in the workshop. Space in the survey needs to be alloted to an open ended question, "What would you like to see in a quality science workshop?" This gives participants a chance to indicate what they personally would want to experience in improving the science curriculum. The following items in the survey, as an example, may be numbered as to importance by each workshop participant :

- computers and technology use in teaching science
- use of science library books in ongoing lesson/unit discussions
- a multi-media emphasis in teaching and learning situations
- engaging learners in ongoing science lessons and units of study
- student self monitoring of achievement
- metacognition strategies in teaching and learning situations (Zahra, 2008).

There needs to be adequate time for participants to appraise the value of the workshop. Feedback is necessary to increase the usefulness of workshops to improve the science curriculum. Science teachers need to feel that inservice education programmes are truly effective to provide students with the best objectives, learning opportunities, and assessment procedures.

Then too, teachers may take science education courses online or at an approved university. The course work may lead to an advanced degree in graduate studies. The degree programme should include course work in educational psychology, science education, and science content. School principals need to publicize university offerings which might well meet the needs of science teachers. The local school library should have a section devoted to journals and teacher education textbooks pertaining to science and science education. A convenient setting for teachers to read the science materials needs to be in the offing (Biddle and Saha, 2006).

The Psychology of Teaching Science

There are selected principles of learning which science teachers need to implement in teaching and learning situations. This must go much beyond the recall level of subject-matter presented by the teacher. Thus, students need to analyze content while engaging in lessons and units of study to separate the relevant from the irrelevant as well as the accurate from the inaccurate. This is needed to provide the best information in the solving of problems. Creative thinking, too, is necessary to come up with novel, new ideas. Innovations come about in society due to creative thinking. Novel, unique ideas are then wanted. The worth of an idea needs assessment and involves evaluation (Cuniff and McMillen).

Creating and developing interest in an ongoing science lesson/unit of study is salient. With interest, students ask questions and explore possible answers. The curious learner is one who will grow in the ability to acquire knowledge, skills, and attitudes. An open mind is willing to venture out into the unknown and find gaps in knowledge and skills with the intent of attempting to close the gap.

Metacognitive skills must be achieved. Here, the student, with teacher help, engages in thinking about thinking. Thus, for example, the student reflects upon how he/she evaluated the worth of an idea or how a problem was identified for solving. Additional examples of metacognition include reflection upon how the student :

- arrived at an answer or solution to a problem
- followed a specific sequence in problem solving following a science experiment with the intent of viewing what was missing in the procedure
- engaged in committee work to make for a successful endeavour.

Meaning is always salient to stress in any learning experience. To understand what was taught is of utmost importance. Otherwise, hazy, vague understandings are not useful in building upon those previous learnings. To extend learnings, meaning must be attached to what has transpired.

Purpose for student learning must also be emphasized. Reasons then are accepted by the student for achieving objectives of instruction. The purpose for each activity in science needs to be clearly stated by the teacher/learner and, hopefully, accepted by the latter (National Research Council, 1989).

REFERENCES

Biddle, Bruce, and Lawrence J. Saha (2006), "How Principals Use. Research," *Educational Leadership*, 63 (6), 72-78.

Cuniff, Patricia A., and Janet K. McMillen (1996), "Field Studies," *The Science Teacher*, 63 (5), 55-60.

Ediger, Marlow (2007), *Science Curriculum and Instruction*. New Delhi, India: Discovery Publishing House.

Ediger, Marlow (2008), "Mental Health in the Curriculum," *Edutracks*, 7 (7),13-15. Published in India.

Ediger, Marlow (2007-2008), "Student Vocabulary Development in Science," *Connecticut Journal of Science Education*, 45 (1), 12-13.

Ediger, Marlow (2008), "Training Staff to Teach Reading in the Content Areas," *Leadership Compass*, 5(3), 1-2. Published by the National Association of Elementary School Principals.

Hansen, Laurie (2003), "Science in Any Language," *Science and Children*, 41 (3), 35-39.

National Research Council (1989), *National Science Standards*. Washington, DC: National Academy Press.

Ohanian, Susan, and Philip Kovacs (2007), "Make Room at the Table for Teachers", 89 (4), 270-274.

Zahra, Anne (2008), "Limitless Images : Digital Photography in the Classroom," *The Delta Kappa Gamma Bulletin*, 75 (1), 7-9, 17.

31

School Principal as Science Supervisor

Science supervision may come from several resource personnel. In the elementary/middle school level, the principal may assume that responsibility. He/she must be well-versed pertaining to trends in science teaching. Continually studying what makes for an effective science curriculum is a must! The principal has numerous opportunities to observe quality science instruction when making observational visits to different classrooms. Ideas gleaned may be passed on to other teachers. The principal needs to not only encourage good science teaching but also must motivate teachers in the school setting to share ideas and assist other teachers to teach effectively and well. Thus, there are several resources to use in developing excellence in the science curriculum (Ediger, 2007).

Criteria for School Administrators to Emphasize

There are several guidelines which school administrators need to stress in working with teachers to improve science instruction. Thus, teachers need to engage pupils in learning. Too many pupils are turned off or fail to achieve in an ongoing lesson. These pupils must be identified and brought into the teaching/learning act. A different kind of learning experience in science may assist to develop interest within these learners to achieve. Teacher observation needs to be utilized to notice which pupils might benefit from these changes (Maheshwari, 2009).

Second, pupils need to make sense pertaining to what was taught. Memorizing meaningless materials for a test has meager benefits for the learner. The learner must understand presented facts, concepts, and generalizations in order to use these as building blocks for ensuing lessons. Meaning exists within the mind of the learner. The teacher's role is to assist pupils to understand and use what was achieved. Meaningful explanations, learning opportunities, and feedback from appraisal results, might well help the pupil to achieve at higher levels. New learnings are built upon those acquired previously. Pupils need to raise questions pertaining to what is not comprehended and thus arrive at meaning in the science curriculum.

Third, the school principal must stress pupil purpose in learning when helping teachers develop skill in teaching. With purpose, reasons exist within the pupil in acquisition of knowledge, skills, and attitudes. A low level of motivation results if a pupil cannot sense reasons for achieving vital scientific information. The teacher may very briefly explain, deductively, the purpose or reason for pupils participating in a given science learning activity. Or, inductively pupils may understand the purpose with a series of questions raised by the teacher as to why a specific science activity is necessary to pursue. Motivation might then well increase (NSTA Reports, 2009).

Fourth, pupils achieve at different levels and possess diverse styles of learning, individually. Thus, the teacher must use concrete (the outdoors, excursions, objects and items), the semi-concrete (video tapes, illustrations, computers, slides, and multi-media in general/as well as abstract (listening, speaking, reading, and writing activities), in providing for individual differences in the classroom. Different ways of grouping pupils for instruction, also, must be emphasized, such as homogeneous, heterogeneous, the class as a whole, committee endeavors, and individual study as means of grouping pupils for instruction (National Research Council, 2000).

Observational Visits in Classrooms

The school principal needs to observe science teachers teach in the classroom. There are numerous recommendations which principals may make as a result of these observational visits. Each recommendation is made in order to improve science instruction. The following observations made should be followed with recommendations for improved instruction:

- few pupils are able to see, clearly, the science experiment being performed. Materials used should be arranged in a place whereby observations by all pupils may readily be made. Small groups, in sequence, may need to observe an experiment at a given time. Readiness for the ensuing experiment must be in evidence so that pupils may relate the ensuing with previous learnings acquired. Otherwise optimal learning may not take place. Jumping too far ahead of pupils makes for frustration in achieving whereas experiments performed which are too easy to comprehend might well make for boredom. Experimentation should fascinate learners and foster an inward desire to learn (Ediger, 2008).
- selected pupils are left out of discussions. There may be too few actively participating and yet all need to be actively engaged in the discussion. The science teacher needs to motivate each pupil to participate. No one should be ridiculed for participating, but rather all should be encouraged. The self-concept is involved in assisting all pupils to be successful in the

discussion setting. The class as a whole as well as small group discussions need to be in the offing. The latter helps more pupils to feel free to participate. The self-confidence of each must be strengthened so all have salient contributions to make (David, 2008).

- some may not wish to participate in an ongoing learning opportunity. These need to be identified and motivated to perform. This must be approached cautiously with feelings of success experienced by these learners. No doubt non-contributors have experienced failure too frequently. It might be, also, that these pupils do not understand what is being taught. Reading activities in science do cause difficulties for some pupils. Word recognition problems and difficulties in fluent reading are hindrances in comprehending ideas being read (Pardo, 2004).
- mainstreamed pupils with different disabilities need to be accepted as humans having much worth. They need encouragement to use talents and abilities possessed. Strengths and hobbies need to be brought into the science curriculum. Subject matter discussed may be brought in to their understanding level in small group sessions. No one should experience rudeness or shunning.

Diagnosis for not understanding relevant facts, concepts, and generalizations must be noted and remedied with appropriate learning activities. No child should fall through the slats. Science literacy for all is needed and each learner should attain optimally.

Using Computer Technology in the Classroom

There are a plethora of ways in which pupils may use computer services in the science curriculum. A dictionary, a thesaurus, an encyclopedia, and the word processor itself are tools for learning in ongoing science lessons and units of study. An electronic portfolio is an excellent means of showing achievement for parents, teachers, school administrators, among other responsible people, to notice a child's sequential progress. Here, the pupil with teacher assistance may select what to enter into the computer to show representative progress in science. In the past portfolios have been used to also show a representative sampling of a pupil's progress, but not with computer use. In an electronic portfolio, the pupil may enter the following dated entries in science :

- a book report related directly to subject matter discussed in an ongoing science unit of study such as on prehistoric life in the Mesozoic Era
- a summary on a video tape viewed such as Hurricanes and Tornados
- conclusions reached from a large group session on invertebrates
- electronic pictures taken for a bulletin board display developed on opaque, transparent, and translucent materials
- a mural made on igneous, sedimentary, and metamorphic rocks
- impressions acquired from a unit on sustainable, non-polluting sources of energy
- a write up on an individual self chosen project made pertaining to magnetism and electricity (Ediger, 2006).

The word processor may be used to keep a running record of diary entries kept for each science unit studied. The daily entries need to be dated and each happening recorded accurately and clearly. This activity can easily move into the direction of pupils doing scientific journals. Beckstead (2009) wrote the following :

> Having my students create science journals doesn't happen during the first week of school. The students need to have

data and other information recorded in their science journals in order to order to be able to create science journals. A good place to start is our rocks and minerals unit. During this unit, students observe different kinds of rocks and do different types of tests on the rocks, go on a rock hunt. . .Alt observations are recorded in their science notebooks.

But we are still not ready to create the journal. Not only does the science have to be taught, but also certain writing and grammar skills have to be taught and developed before students write articles, stories, and poems for a science journal.

The science journal is used, along with other procedures, to appraise learner progress in science. Parents, the school principal, the involved pupil, and the science teacher may use the science journal not only to assess but also to report learner progress. Continuous efforts must be made in using modern technology to assist pupils in achieving more optimally in science.

The science teacher always needs to be on the lookout for ways to incorporate computer technology into the science curriculum. It might well be a motivator for learning involving pupils.

Evaluation of Achievement in Science

The school principal has numerous responsibilities as curriculum supervisor to inform teachers on methods of appraising pupil achievement. Thus, he/she needs to assist teachers to understand the following concepts :

- **validity** : Examples need to be given here in that a test is valid if it measures what it is supposed to measure. Thus, if x is to be measured in pupil achievement, the test items then must relate directly to x.
- **reliability** : Here, a test must measure consistently and not fluctuate in test results for a pupil from one testing to the next for the same test. Test/retest, as well as split half reliability, may also be stressed.

- **standard deviation :** This indicates how pupil's test scores deviate from the mean. One standard deviation above the mean represents 34.13 per cent of those taking the test, whereas 34.13 per cent of pupils are below the mean of the total number tested being one standard deviation below the mean.
- **percentiles :** Percentiles show the range of pupil's test scores from the first to the 99th percentile. Thus, for example, if a pupil received a hypothetical score of 36, he/she would be on the 60th percentile; out of every 100 pupils taking the test, forty would be above and sixty below that hypothetical score. The raw score of 36 was compared to a table which gave the percentile results for that test.

The above-named four measurement concepts are used very commonly in mandated testing whereby the mean of all scores is tabulated as well as the standard deviation and percentiles. Percentiles do not mean the per cent answered correctly by a pupil on a test but rather, but rather how he/she compares with others when converting a raw score to a standard score (National Science Education Standards, 1996).

REFERENCES

Beckstead, Larissa (2009), "Scientific Journals, A Creative Assessment Tool," *Science and Children*, 46 (3), 22-23.

David, Jane (2008), "Project Based Learning," *Educational Leadership*, 65 (5), 80-84.

Ediger, Marlow (2006), "Testing Versus Portfolios to Assess Achievement," *OASCD Journal*, 13(1), 31-32.

Ediger, Marlow (2007), *School Science Education*. New Delhi, India: Discovery Publishing House.

Ediger, Marlow (2008), "Leadership in the School Setting," *Education*, 129 (1), 17-20.

Maheshwari, Amrita (2009), "Integral Values of Science Education," *Edutracks*, 8 (4), 16-17.

National Research Council (2000), *How Pupils Learn.* Washington, DC: National Academy Press.

National Science Education Standards (1996), National Research Council (NRC). Washington, DC: National Academy Press.

NSTA Reports (2009), National Science Teachers Association. Washington DC: NSTA.

Pardo, Laura (2004), "What Every Teacher Needs to Know About Comprehension," *The Reading Teacher*, 58 (3), 272-283.

32

Decision-making in Science Curriculum

There are numerous worthwhile objectives for pupils to achieve in science. Knowledge objectives are salient for learner achievement, but equally important are skills ends. Perhaps, the two kinds of objectives cannot be separated from each other. Knowledge is used when making choices, from among alternative subject matter which might be studied. Then too, knowledge decisions are used to solve problems. Thus, facts, concepts, and generalizations are chosen to find solutions.

Being able to make decisions is very useful in school settings where short and more long terms choices are made such as friendships versus possible vocational choices. In the science curriculum, choices might also be stressed in terms of which objectives to pursue, learning opportunities to engage in, as well as choices in assessment procedures, from among others. Ongoing science lessons and units of study provide ample opportunities for decisions making (Ediger2007).

Decision-making in Science

The science teacher needs to be well versed in styles of learning and how to provide for individual differences among learners.

Using learning centres is one method to emphasize to encourage pupils in making choices from among alternatives. One or more centers, teacher determined or through teacher/pupil planning, may then be put into place in a classroom. If one learning center is developed by the science teacher, then enrichment learnings may be stressed. The teacher develops a task card suggesting possibilities for choosing a learning activity. Materials to use are also available at the center. Here, pupils, for example, may choose to make models of prehistoric life from clay or play-dough. Or at a more complex level, depending upon learners readiness, a pupil may choose to do a written report on plants and animals in the Mesozoic Era.

Several learning centres might also be developed. Thus, five or six centres, each containing four tasks listed on a card provide choices for pupils to select and complete individually or in a small group endeavour. In a science unit on changes in the earth's surface, pupils, here, may select to work at the following stations, as examples :

- a hurricane/tornado center whereby pupils may view related video tapes on this topic and do a written/oral report to the class on their findings.
- a soil erosion centre indicating the effects of wind/water on soil. Ways of preventing and minimizing these effects should also be studied with the use of different reference sources such as the internet. Models may be made to show counteractions to prevent soil erosion with the planting of trees and grass.
- drawings might well be completed on causes of earthquakes. Pupils may use science encyclopedias, among other reference sources, to secure necessary information.with the results posted on the classroom bulletin board (Blough and Schwartz, 1984).

It was noticed when supervising university student teachers in the public schools that a few teachers used learning centers for an entire science unit of study. Others used a few centers to supplement the regular science curriculum whereas some used one center for enrichment purposes. When making decisions in using a learning centers procedure, the following need consideration :

- how well pupils are learning when using this approach. Do they achieve objectives well in a decision-making procedure of learning?
- are pupils responsible individuals in an informal approach to learning?
- do pupils use the methods the of science when participating in decision making in doing science activities and experiences?
- are learners showing respect and acceptance of others? (Booker, 2008).

Decision-making by pupils may also be stressed when carefully chosen science textbooks are used as a guide for lessons and units of study taught. Thus within a lesson, pupils might identify a problem for solving. The problems is relevant and must be clearly stated so it can be solved. Deliberation is necessary. An hypothesis is developed as a tentative answer to the identified problem. Various reference sources are used to gather information to test the tentative hypothesis.

Projects may also be chosen as a result of pupils being engaged in reading/discussing ideas from the basal science textbook. The project may involve individual or committee work such as making models, taking an excursion and summarizing its findings, as well as constructing objects and items related directly to the ongoing unit of study (National Science Education Standards, 1996).

Discussion groups may also be formed whereby peers gather information and discuss alternative forms of energy such as solar, geothermal, and wind. A detailed set of conclusions may be drawn up to evaluate the quality of the findings/discussion. In committee work, it is important for all to participate and no one dominate in the different interactions. Ideas need to be stated clearly as individuals participate.

Reading across the curriculum might truly be stressed when basal textbooks are used in science teaching and learning. When reading content, pupils may be assisted in phonics, use of context clues, onset and rimes in word pronunciation, as well as prefixes and suffixes in identification of words (Ediger, 1996).

Learnings may certainly be extended when basals are used. Library book and internet sources may be integrated into the ongoing unit of study when basal science texts are utilized. Extended learnings are emphasized when :

- it adds to meaningful science facts, concepts, and generalizations
- it assists pupils to develop indepth interests in science through problem solving, project methods, and discussions
- it provides for individual differences such as abilities and talents of learners
- it varies the kinds of learning opportunities provided for pupils in he classroom setting.

Toward the other end of the continuum in a more formal science curriculum, the teacher may select science objectives which are measurably stated for pupils to attain. These may come from mandated objectives on the state level. The objectives deal with knowledge ends largely. The objectives are precisely written and pupils do/do not achieve them as a result of teaching. Learning activities are then aligned with the stated objectives. Test results may be machine scored and one correct answer for each multiple choice test item is possible. Each pupil's results are indicated numerically as in percentiles, standard deviations, and grade equivalents.

Unless the teacher invites, there is little leeway to emphasize questions from learners, discussion groups, and project development (Beckstead, 2008).

Testing is a major way of determining what pupils have learned in a formal approach of teaching. With test scores from pupil test results, the teacher may notice how well learners are achiving. With mandated tests, the results from testing of different classrooms and schools, comparisons can be made to notice the quality of achievement. Are pupils doing better than previously? Teachers might well be held accountable for these test resuts. Accountability is then being emphasized. Pertaining to accountability, Johnson and Bonaiuto (2009) wrote the following :

> Accountability is the catalyst that drives educational progress. But if accountability does not grow out of a local context, with roots in what the community values, it loses meaning.

Too frequently, educators rely on test scores as the primary measure of how well a school is doing. Externally mandated data rather than community priorities shape the public conversation about education. Newspapers publish school rankings, parents look to see how their child stacks up, and teachers are able to handle community pressures centered on test scores with no other measure as a balance.

There are numerous methods of evaluation, in addition to testing, which may be used to ascertain learner achievement and progress. These include :

- teacher observation. He/she may observe how well pupils interact with each other in committee work such as staying on task and respecting each other.
- anecdotal records. The science teacher records and dates specific observations made as in pupils doing a project such as making a model solar collector. Accuracy, cooperation, neatness, and acceptance of others are important observations to make. Interviews

with pupils also provide information for anecdotal records.

- self-evaluation. Here, pupils may respond with ratings on a five point scale to such items as—relies upon the self for task completion, interacts well with others, and assists others as needed

REFERENCES

Beckstead, Larissa (2008), "Scientific Journals," *Science and Children*, 46 (3), 22-26.

Booker, Keonya (2008), "The Role of Peers and Instructors in Establishing a Classroom Community," *Journal of Instructional Psychology*, 35 (1), 12-16.

Blough, Glenn, and Julius Schwartz (1984), *Elementary School Science and How to Teach It*. New York: CBS Publishing Company.

Ediger, Marlow (2007) *School Science Education*. New Delhi, India: Discovery Publishing House.

Ediger, Marlow (1996), "Activity Centered Versus Subject Centered Curriculum," *The Educational Review*, 102 (1),17-20.

Johnson, George, and Susan Bonaiuto (2009), "Accountability With Roots," *Educational Leadership*, 66 (4), 26-29.

National Science Education Standards (1996), National Research Council. Washington, DC: Academy Press.

33

Psychology of Learning and Science Curriculum

The psychology of learning is important to emphasize in teaching science since pupil achievement is then optimized. There are selected standards then which are stressed in teaching and learning situations. Interest, as one factor, is salient to stress so that pupils are on task in going lessons and learning opportunities (Gilbert and Kotelman, 2005). Which standards from the psychology of learning should then be inherent in teaching science?

Learning Opportunities to Achieve Objectives

To achieve relevant, salient objectives in science, pupils need to experience quality instruction. Quality in instruction emphasizes teacher use of education psychology to assist pupil progress. Thus, meaning theory should be stressed continuously as pupils acquire vital science facts, concepts, and generalizations. Pupil need to be able to explain what has been achieved. Merely memorizing or parroting back what the science teacher has explained does not stress learning. Rather, the pupil should be able to explain in his/her own words what the acquired content means. Thus, the learner is in a better position to build upon previous learnings when participating in an ensuing experience. A connection needs to exist between the old and new ideas gleaned. Further, relationships must be formed between the pupil and his/her personal experiences. Thus, the science curriculum needs to be related to functional experiences of the learner. What has been learned or is being learned must be useful in school and in society. Science needs to be connected, also, to other branches of knowledge such as mathematics which is the language of science (Ediger, 2007).

Behaviorism, as a school of psychology, emphasizes that precise, measurably stated objectives need to be determined for classroom teaching. The science teacher must emphasize relevant, precise objectives, written, for pupils to achieve. The degree of precision generally will make it so that pupils either do/do not achieve the objective. Measurability is salient here. E. L. Thorndike (1874-1949) believed that whatever exists, exists in some amount, and if it exists, it can be measured. Tests are then developed to measure what is stated in the objective. Standardized tests fit this pattern to measure what exists. Here, pupils on a certain grade level take the same test, within the same allotted time, using the same directions in taking the test. Validity and reliability data are provided in the standardized test's manual which makes it possible to compare one's own pupil's results with those in the norm group. The norm group who took the test and their results provided data on what one's own pupils would rank percentile wise. If, for example, a pupil in the science teacher's classroom received a raw score of 60 on the standardized science test, this would equal the 75th percentile, as shown in the Manual (Marice, 2005).

Much effort and expense go into the development of a standardized test. The science teacher may write his/her own test based upon the objectives emphasized in class. He/she is also teaching toward ends or objectives which pupils are to achieve. Diagnosis is involved if the science teacher analyzes data from these tests to notice what needs reteaching. There are a plethora of reasons for a pupil not having secured a correct answer such as :

- not having understood what was being taught
- sequence in learning was not in evidence
- not having paid attention to ongoing learning experiences
- not being on task
- not participating actively in an ongoing lesson (Condrey, 1996).

The science teacher may also appraise his/her own teaching by looking back at what might have caused learners to make these errors. A different teaching strategy may need to be implemented in order to guide optimal learner achievement.

Behaviorism then stresses the use of precise objectives in teaching where there is agreement among educators as to what pupils are to learn within each stated objective. Tests must be aligned with the stated objectives. Valid and reliable tests then should convey what pupils have learned as a result of testing.

Somewhat opposite of behaviorism is humanism as a psychology of education. A. H. Maslow's (1954) hierarchy of needs is salient to stress here. Maslow indicated five levels of meeting pupil needs in the total development of the individual. These are :

- meeting the physiological needs of pupils such as adequate food, clothing, and shelter.
- taking care of safety needs of pupils including physical and mental safety such as freedom from harassment, emotional, and social abuse.
- belonging needs in that pupils desire to belong to and be accepted within groups. Rejection is a negative feeling.
- esteem needs. Here, the pupil wishes to receive recognition for accomplishment and achievement.

Being ignored or ridiculed does not meet the esteem needs criteria.

- becoming the kind of person desired.

The individual is viewed holistically when studying the above named criteria.

Humanism emphasizes decision making and choices in terms of what to learn, and this is stressed within a framework. There are several plans available to stress humanism in the science curriculum. One plan is the contract agreed upon by the pupils with teacher assistance. Here, the pupil decides upon what he/she wishes to complete within a designated time, which may be modified if need be. Thus from an ongoing science unit of study, the pupil, for example, agrees to complete the following :

- do three activities from the enrichment center
- read a library book and summarize its findings
- view a video tape and develop a related model
- do four science experiments and draw relevant conclusions.

The contract is signed by the pupils and by the teacher with the due date provided. All completed work is to show effort and neatness. The plan is developed by the involved learner and has teacher supervision. Evaluation of the products involve both pupil and teacher.

Carl Rogers (1983) was a leading advocate of using humanism as a psychology of learning. As a young boy, he had a unique interest in moths. Fortunately, his primary grade teacher shared and encourage this personal interest. Rogers (1983) believed children were naturally curious about their environment and extended and developed interests in depth. Pupils should then try out their very own ideas without fear of ridicule or facing rude comments. Self-directed learning and choosing what to learn are salient. Being a motivated pupil increases as he/she select what to pursue. Implications here for the science teacher are the following :

- assist pupils to choose their own purposes in learning
- guide pupils to become responsible learners
- promote life-long learning by having pupils select what is interesting to learn and engages each learner.

Humanism then focuses upon the individual pupil in the teaching and learning process. Small group and committee learning are to be emphasized if based on learner interests. Vygotsky (1933, 1978) stressed the importance of cooperative learning whereby pupils interact with each other in ideas expressed and growth in achievement comes about in a social situation. Ideas then "bounce off the minds of pupils" as they pursue a concept or generalization.

Constructivism in the Science Curriculum

Constructivism, as a psychology of learning, is also pupil centered. Pupils then are actively involved in selecting, with teacher assistance, what to learn in ongoing units of study. Sequence resides within the pupil, not the teacher. The learner sequences what comes next in pursuing an activity or a project. The learner makes connections between preceding experiences and the ensuing science lesson/unit of study. Questions from pupils are encouraged so that gaps in learning may be minimized. These gaps are perceived when a pupil does not perceive closure between the known and the unknown in ensuing science subject matter being studied. Questions are also asked when curiosity is inherent in wondering about specifics in the natural environment, such as having seen dew on grass in the morning on a nice spring day, adjacent to the school. The learner then wants to know why dew occurs. This may expand to performing science experiments to show causes of dew in the natural environment. Curiosity of pupils must be motivated so that pupils develop attitudes necessary for achieving objectives in the science curriculum (National Science Education Standards, 1996).

Problem identification by pupils is salient for a constructivist emphasis in teaching and learning situations. John Dewey (1916) was an early advocate of using problem solving methods of teaching. Within a science unit, pupils select a problem area which requires deliberation, critical, and creative thinking. An hypothesis is developed in response to the problem. The hypothesis needs testing with the use of experimentation, the internet, science encyclopedias, among others, as information sources. The hypothesis is then refuted, modified, or accepted as is.

Within a problem-solving activity, pupils with teacher guidance, are actively involved in identification of the problem, developing an hypothesis, as well as choosing a variety of reference sources to use in its evaluation. These processes are ordered and sequenced by involved learners.

Project methods are also pupil-centred. This method was developed by William Heard Kilpatrick (1918). He emphasized pupil purposing, pupil planning, pupils caring out the plan, and pupil evaluation of the product. The project method is very salient presently as a method of teaching whereby the learner is heavily involved in the total process. Thus the pupil, for example, individually or collectively determine a project such as developing models of as well as a chart showing classifications of vertebrates and invertebrates. Both need carefully planning in order to complete quality products. Adherence to a well developed plan makes for meticulous work among involved learners. Approved criteria are developed and used to appraise the final product. Here, pupils, too, sequence their very own work, as is typical of constructivism as a psychology of learning.

IN CONCLUSION

Tenets from the psychology of learning need to be studied and implemented to assist pupils to achieve more optimally. Pupils possess different styles of learning. The following are preferences which pupils have pertaining to their individual method of processing information and skills :

- a structured science curriculum as compared to one being more open-ended
- teacher selection of learning opportunities for pupils as compared to learners largely sequencing their own experiences
- teachers appraising learner achievement, or pupils being heavily involved in the assessment process.

REFERENCES

Condrey, Jean Friend (1996), "Focus on Science Concepts," *The Science Teacher*, 63 (4), 23-28.

Dewey, John (1916), *Democracy and Education*. New York : Macmillan Company.

Ediger, Marlow (2007), *School Science Education*. New Delhi, India : Discovery Publishing House.

Gilbert, Joan, and Marleen Kottelman (2007), "Five Good Reasons to Use Science Notebooks," *Science and Children*, 43 (3), 28-32.

Kilpatrick, William Heard (1918), *The Project Method*. New York: Teacher's College, Columbia University.

Marice, P. V. (2005), Problem Solving Ability, Aptitude and Competency in Science Trainees In Colleges of Education in Kerala. Ph D., University of Madras, Chennai, India.

Maslow, A. H. (1954) *Motivation and Personality*. New York: Harper and Row.

National Science Education Standards (1996), National Research Council. Washington DC: Academy Press.

Rogers, Carl (1983), *Freedom to Learn: A View of What Education Might Become*. Columbus, Ohio: Charles Merrill Company.

Vygotsky, Len S. (1933-1978), *Mind in Society: The Development of Higher Psychological Processes*. Cambridge, Massachusetts: Harvard University Press.

34

Motivating Students in Science Curriculum

Motivating students to learn is continually important in teaching and learning situations, science being no exception. Motivated students are easier to teach and do achieve more optimally. The science teacher must select relevant objectives for pupils to attain. There needs to be balance among knowledge, skills, and attitudinal objectives. Each is salient. Knowledge ends pertain to vital science facts, concepts, and generalizations for learners to acquire, inductively as well as deductively. Skills emphasize using content from the knowledge objectives. Attitudinal ends are on outgrowth of learning activities stressed for pupils in achieving the desired knowledge and skills objectives.

Factors Involved in Motivating Pupils

There are a plethora of factors involved in motivation. First, pupils need to be engaged in an ongoing learning experience. In a science unit on classification of animals, pupils may observe fish in the classroom aquarium. Many characteristics of fish may be noticed such as how they move, how they breathe and stay under water, and what they eat. Illustrations shown further clarifies concepts pertaining to fish. Motivated pupils secure much knowledge from observations made. Questions raised and discussions held further elaborate on vital ideas pertaining to fish. Meticulous observations made objectively are characteristics of a good scientist! A chart may be developed of observations made, showing characteristics of vertebrates classified as fish. To branch out for further learning activities, pupils might be guided to develop a scrapbook, individually or in a committee, of different kinds of fish and their accompanying pictures. Reading science subject matter is another good way to attain necessary information. All experiences need to be challenging and success oriented (Ediger and Rao, 2003).

Second, pupils need to experience background information to understand new learnings. In classifying a second category of vertebrates, pupils should study amphibians. During the spring months, pupils might study tadpoles swimming in a jar. As they mature, tadpoles become more like frogs. Direct observation, again, is salient to notice these changes in time. Pupils should keep a journal of changes occurring from tadpoles in water to frogs on land. Illustrations drawn by pupils should accompany the respective write-up. The internet should be used to gather information, in depth, pertaining to amphibians, to check direct observations made. Library book content may provide further information on amphibians (Cuniff and McMillen, 1996).

Third, learners need to study the category of reptiles. These can be quite diverse in their representation and include snakes, turtles, alligators, and crocodiles. To become and remain motivated, pupils must attach meaning and understand what is taught and learned. A power point presentation may pin-point specific features for each reptile named above and assist in making learnings meaningful. Individually, or in committees, pupils may list features which distinguish reptiles from amphibians and fish. Likenesses also need to be explored such as being cold-blooded. The listings need to be compared and accurate conclusions drawn. A variety of reference sources may be used to corroborate or refute findings. Objectivity is a key element in learning (Horejsi 2003).

Fourth, birds provide a fourth category of invertebrates. Here, the science teacher may have pupils look outdoors to see different kinds of birds. A bird feeder located outside the classroom window attracts blue jays, cardinals, sparrows, and finches. Pupils tend to be fascinated with birds in the out of doors. They notice and discuss their characteristics. Pupils are interested in knowing that this is the first category of vertebrates which are warm blooded and whose body temperature is much higher than that of human beings. During the school year, they notice which birds migrate such as robins. Pupils learn which birds eat seeds, insects, or both kinds of feed. A comparison chart was developed by separate committees to show how birds differ from reptiles, frogs, and fish. A video tape was then played showing these comparisons and pupils could check their charted hypotheses from that in the video tape. A lively discussion followed pertaining vertebrates read about pertaining to other regions in the world. The duck billed platypus of Australia has characteristics of both birds and mammals. Pupils need to think critically when separating these categories and why they possess similarities and differences. Critical thinking is a major objective in teaching science (National Research Centre, 1996).

Next, mammals need to be studied in ongoing lessons and in a unit of study, together with other vertebrates. Many children have a pet cat or dog as a source of information. The basal text contains illustrations and subject-matter on diverse mammals, as well as other categories of vertebrates. The illustrations need to be studied to provide pupils with background information for reading the ensuing content. The new words to be encountered may be printed on the chalkboard for pupil viewing and discussing. They might also be shown on a screen projected by a computer. The new words may then be identified by pupils when reading the assigned subject-matter. Readiness for reading by possessing background information and by being able to identify the new words in print is salient. Pupils will raise questions prior to the reading activity on mammals. These questions may be printed on a flip chart for pupils to secure needed information while reading. The new words may also be printed on a word wall for future reference. Answers to questions might well be a follow-up activity. The teacher may identify additional questions and problems for discussion. Problems take time in identifying an hypothesis to be tested with the use of additional reference sources for further study and analysis (Blough and Schwartz 1984).

When reading science content, pupils need to monitor their comprehension individually to notice if meaning and understanding is occurring and not word calling only. By rehearsing subject matter read, pupils realize if comprehension is occurring. Two pupils reading the same content from the basal may listen to each other explain subject matter read. In this way, both become more conscious of content comprehended, Metacognitive strategies, acquired by pupils, helps learners to reflect upon what has been read to ascertain if :

- ideas read possessed clarity.
- content is nebulous and needs more indepth study.
- improved reading strategies might be used, if so which ones?
- different word attack skills need to be used.
- critical thought needs to be used pertaining to a conclusion reached.
- creative thinking is necessary to explore novel ideas (Fitzburgh, 2006).

Creative thinking stresses pupils coming up with unique ideas in ongoing discussions. Poetry, in particular emphasizes originality of thought and making novel comparisons. Science content studied may be transposed into different kinds of verse written by pupils. In this way, pupils use science subject matter studied. Thus, pupils need to attach meaning to and write free verse :

- fish breathe through gills, not lungs
  use the tail and fins to propel motion
  live in water, not on land
  swim rapidly to secure food and avoid enemies
  lay eggs to provide offspring.
- rhymed verse may include a quatrain, containing four lines with alternate lines of rhyme
  amphibians live part of their lives in water
  they also live on land
  amphibians begin life with gills, then lungs later
  and may live on sand.

Additional kinds of rhyme include couplets (two lines of rhymed verse); triplets with three lines of rhymed verse; and limericks whereby lines one, two, and five rhyme with lines three and four rhyming.

- poetry containing a selected number of syllables per line, such as haiku with its five, seven, five progression of syllables per line :
  Cold blooded turtles
  They live on both land and sea
  Their young hatch from eggs.

Many pupils, when ready, like to experiment with writing different kinds of poetry (Tiedt, 1982). They find it fascinating to put science knowledge to use in a creative manner and this should aid in retention of subject matter. There are a variety of ways to use content learned in addition to those discussed previously and include the following :

- self evaluation of subject matter acquired
- teacher evaluation of pupil achievement, such as in anecdotal statements

- charts developed to show the progression of stages in each category of vertebrates
- scrapbooks containing illustrations of each category of vertebrates with vital subject matter explaining each
- making models of vertebrates from paper mache, and/ or paper toweling of fish, snakes, turtles, birds, and mammals. When supervising university student teachers, the writer noticed these kinds of models made by sixth graders and then suspended with string from the classroom ceiling.
- developing an individual portfolio (See Bowers, 2005).

As pupils make these models, they ask questions about vertebrates and seek more related information. *Motivation* to learn is then indeed high!

REFERENCES

Blough, Glenn O., and Julius Schwartz (1984), *Elementary School Science and How to Teach It.* New York: CBS College Publishing.

Bowers, Susan P. (2005), "The Portfolio Process: Questions for Implementation and Practice," *College Student Journal*, 39 (4), 753-758.

Cuniff, Patricia A., and Janet K. McMillen (1996), "Field Studies," *The Science Teacher*, 63:51.

Ediger, Marlow, and D. Bhaskara Rao (2003), *Teaching Science in the Elementary School.* New Delhi, India: Discovery Publishing House.

Fitzburgh, Will (2006), "Where's the Content?" *Educational Leadership*, 64 (2), 42-47.

Horejsi, Martin (2003), "Making Technology Inclusive," *Science and Children*, 41 (3), 20-24.

National Research Center (1996), *National Science Education Standards. Washington*, DC: National Academy Press.

Tiedt, Iris M. (1982), The Language Arts Handbook. Prentice-Hall, Inc., Englewood Cliffs, New Jersey.

35

Data Driven Decision-making in Science

Data driven decision-making is based upon more objective models of instruction than is usually the case. Thus, there is evidence available to make choices in terms of future actions in school improvement. This may be compared to using hunches, feelings, and the affective domain in decision making. Not that feelings are all bad; there are feelings involved in any action taken in life. For example, in buying a used car, the shopper may evaluate the price of three desired automobiles and make objective comparisons here. Perhaps, they are quite uniform in quality. The buyer, though, prefers one color as compared to the others. That preference is based upon the affective domain only or largely. The buyer does not know how well each of the three cars will perform in the future. It might be the one chosen does the poorest and has the largest personal expenditures for repairs.

In pupil achievement and progress in the classroom, data driven decisions have their advantages. Thus, there is information available for choosing from among alternatives in arriving at the best decisions for assisting pupils to develop and grow (Marice, 2005).

Decision-making in the Curriculum

The science teacher needs to be systematic in selecting those learning opportunities which guide pupil optimal progress. Thus, information might well be considered whereby numerical results tip the scales in terms of choosing pupil activities.

Mandated tests are given quite frequently in the public schools such as in grades three through eight. These are generally standardized tests. A national, reputable company has developed these tests which have been pilot tested and have accompanying norms. The pupils in the local school take these tests on their respective grade levels. The raw score an individual obtains is identified with the same score in the accompanying manual of the test which then gives the equivalent percentile or grade equivalent. The percentile given, for example, may be the 35th percentile, meaning that out of every 100 pupils taking the test, 35 are below and 65 are above that raw score received by the learner.

When viewing the results on the separate test items, the science teacher makes decisions on what is needed for the pupil to achieve sequentially and more optimally. If pupils missed answers pertaining to the following concepts—igneous, sedimentary, and metamorphic rocks-the science teacher needs to provide learning activities to assist pupils to understand and attach meaning to these concepts, using concrete, semi-concrete, and abstract experiences for pupils. Diagnosis and remediation might well be in evidence here. Data is then used in teacher decision making (Ediger, 2007).

Teacher written tests, such as multiple choice tests, also provide data to make decisions. Each test item, generally, must have a stem with four distractors, one of which is clearly the correct answer. The stem with each distractor should be grammatically correct so that no clues are given as to which of the four is the correct answer. It is important to have all distractors of similar length so that the pupil's focus is on the possible correct answer and not to second guess as to which is correct due to its length. Teacher written tests can be strongly valid if face validity is stressed. Thus, the science teacher may write a multiple choice test item for each concept or generalization taught. Reliability may be a problem in that test results vary from one testing to the next of the same test. This would indicate test/retest reliability is emphasized. Generally or even rarely, does the teacher give the same test again to secure information on its reliability such as test/retest reliability. Standardized tests do provide reliability data in their respective manual. They are set up to do that and must, due to tests needing to measure consistently if they possess worth. For example, if a pupil received a score of fifteen correct on a fifty item test and the next time received a score of forty five correct on the same test, the question arises as to what level is the pupil truly achieving. To run a test/retest correlation by giving the same teacher written test twice to the same pupils would waste valuable teaching time in the classroom. Or writing alternate forms of a test to check reliability is not feasible since it takes time and revisions to write these two forms of equal difficulty as well as run tests to take out weaknesses to have high quality results on reliability. For the science teacher who writes a valid multiple choice test, he/she may check reliability of that test by using split half reliability. Thus, the odd numbered are compared with the even numbered test item results, by using the Pearson Product Moment correlation. A measurement or computer specialist in the local school can run the answer sheets of pupil responses through a computer to obtain correlations. The higher the numerical results obtained for the correlation, the stronger the relationship is between the odd versus the even numbered ideas. Thus, a correlation of .80 is much superior to a correlation of .20 when comparing responses for the odd versus even numbered responses for a teacher written test. If computer services are not available to run correlations between odd versus even numbered responses, the science teacher may scan visually by noticing the consistency of responses for each pupil in the classroom to secure a rough estimate of split half reliability of test results (National Science Teachers Association, 2001).

The science teacher needs to reflect upon pupil test results to measure science achievement. The following questions then need to be answered :

- did the test truly measure what was taught? This is a question which refers to the validity of the measurement instrument?
- were important subject matter learnings covered in the test?
- are the test items written with clarity so that misunderstandings do not occur of inherent meanings of each item to the test taker?
- were vaguely written, ambiguous test items removed or rewritten?
- according to the print out of test results, which test items did pupils answer incorrectly? Should these be retaught? Diagnosis and remediation are involved in this question.
- what do the test results imply for successful teaching?
- do the responses leave leeway for guessing? If so, lower reliability in the measurement instrument will accrue (Brady, 2008).
- were the test data adequate to assist in making curricular decisions in science?

Data-driven decision-making depends upon using objective information to improve teaching and learning situations. Metacognitive reflection by the science teacher pertaining to test writing as well as all facets of teaching should assist in improving the curriculum. Too frequently, teachers fail to rethink what pupils experienced in science. Modification of teaching practices might well be necessary in order that each pupil achieves more optimally.

With standardized testing, the time limits for test taking are the same for all fifth graders, for example, and others of the same grade level. The directions give for test taking are the same, and the same key, of course, is use to check test scores (Kelly, 2008).

Essay testing presents more of a problem to provide objective data, as compared to multiple choice tests. However, rubric development and use in scoring essay items tends to make the results more objective. A rubric, ideally, provides standards for scoring, generally on a five point scale for each test item to be appraised. For example in doing a science experiment on a five point scale, to receive a five - the highest rating a pupil may be evaluated on each of the following through teacher observation :

- observes the experiment carefully without jumping to hasty conclusions
- formulates an hypothesis based on observation
- secures information from a variety of reference sources to check the hypothesis
- modifies the hypothesis if necessary
- if need be, tests the new hypothesis.

The rubric results may be used as data to improve science teaching and learning. Each of the five component parts provides feedback to the science teacher in planning ensuing lessons and units of study. Weaknesses might then be remedied.

The write up of the science experiment or other written work might well require a different rubric (Ediger, 2009). The following criteria may be developed and used to appraise written products :

- expresses ideas accurately
- uses complete sentences in writing
- sentences are written sequentially

- correct spelling of words is in evidence
- subject and predicate agree in number.

In reading science subject-matter, the teacher may record the kinds of errors made by pupils and use the data to inform decision making for ensuing lessons. Thus for example in reading from the science basal, a pupil may fail to identify the word "igneous". The science teacher may list this word on a 5 × 8 inch card and provide practice for the pupil in word mastery. This should assist the learner in correctly identifying the word and knowing its contextual meaning. There are diverse kinds of specific errors pupils make in reading and these provide objectives for a future lesson :

- reading haltingly which hinders fluency in comprehension of content
- omitting words or making substitutions for the correct word
- not paying attention to punctuation marks such as commas, periods, question marks, and exclamation points
- failure in using proper stress, pitch, and enunciation
- repeating words read correctly (Ediger, 2008).

Each of the above kinds of errors needs recording which provide feedback to the science teacher to improve comprehension in reading science content. Remedying difficulties might well help the pupil to develop an improved self concept for learning. Data driven decisions help to objectify the selection of objectives which pupils need to achieve.

IN CLOSING

Science teachers need quality information which guide decision making in teaching and learning situations. Guesswork is then minimized in the decision-making arena.

Good decisions are made based on the best kind of information possible.

REFERENCES

Brady, Marion (2008), "Cover the Material—Or Teach Students to Think?" *Educational Leadership*, 65 (5), 64-67.

Ediger, Marlow (2009), "Oral Communication in Science Teaching," *Experiments in Education*, 37 (1), 17-20.

Ediger, Marlow (2007), *School Science Education*. New Delhi, India: Discovery Publishing House.

Ediger, Marlow (2008), "Leadership in the School Setting," *Education*, 129(1),17-20.

Kelly, William E. (2008), "Psychometric Properties and Correlates of the Robert Morris Attention Scale," *Reading Improvement*, 45 (1), 19-25.

Marice, F. W. (2005), Problem Solving Ability, Aptitude, Attitude, and Competency in Teaching Science Trainees in Colleges of Education in Kerala. Ph D., University of Madras, India.

National Science Teacher Association (2001), *Classroom Assessment and the National Education Standards*. Washington, DC: NSTA.

36

Readiness for Learning in Science

Readiness is an important factor in learning. This is true of any lesson and unit of study in science. The science teacher must make decisions pertaining to prerequisites which have/have not been mastered prior to stressing pupils achieving a new objective. If pupils are not ready for the ensuing learnings, they will experience frustration. New objectives must be challenging and yet be achievable by the learner. Enjoyment and excitement in learning are salient in science to make for more optimal progress.

The science teacher must be well prepared for each day of teaching so that pupils might attain relevant objectives, experience stimulating learning activities, as well as quality evaluation techniques which provide feedback to the teacher as well as pupils to improve the curriculum (Ediger, 2007).

Readiness and the Learner

How is readiness secured within pupils? One salient factor is to have learners possess adequate background information in order to benefit from ensuing experiences. Thus, in order to benefit from a unit on magnetism and electricity, pupils need selected understandings. The teacher, depending upon the maturation level of involved pupils, may have different materials in paper cups such as bits of paper, wood, steel nails, marbles, and cereal. Pupils individually might then hypothesize which items from the separate cups will be attracted by a bar or horse shoe magnet. Responses need to be recorded.

Additional readiness may be emphasized such as testing a suspended bar magnet from string with another magnet to determine if like poles attract or repel. Most pupils enjoy these activities. They also like to experiment with magnets on their own. These experiences, among others, provide readiness for pupils to benefit more fully from the new unit on magnetism and electricity. With needed prerequisite learnings, pupils are better able to achieve challenging objectives of instruction. The readiness experiences need to harmonize sequentially with the new learnings to be acquired. A seamless science curriculum is an end result (Gilbert and Kotelman, 2005).

In addition to having met readiness prerequisites, pupils also must perceive purpose in and for an ensuing unit of study. Purpose for learning resides within the pupil, not within the teacher. The latter assists in setting the stage for pupils perceiving purpose or reasons for learning. Reasons for attaining objectives then are in evidence. To perceive purpose, the pupil needs to become engaged in ongoing learning activities and intrinsically accept reasons for active participation. The teacher may briefly explain a purpose for the ensuing lesson, for example, by stating why pupils need to experience a unit on electricity and magnetism. This may be done, for example, by indicating how magnets pick up heavy loads of metal to be loaded onto a truck. The principle here of opposite poles attract is being emphasized such as a north pole attracting a south pole. If a teacher stated purpose does not motivate, then having pupils hypothesize reasons for learning about magnets might well be stressed. Generally, pupils come up with one or more reasons (National Research Council, 1996).

Third, pupils must experience interest in learning as a readiness factor. Interest propels pupil achieving of objectives of instruction. The learning opportunity and the learner become one and not separated from each other. If separation of the two occur, then perhaps little learning takes place. Hopefully, the pupil will become interested to the point that wholehearted involvement is in evidence. There are times when a pupil may desire to have the time extended for learning and achievement in science. Interest is a vital criterion to stress in science learning. When supervising university student teachers in the public schools, the writer has noticed primary grade pupils huddled around an aquarium discussing the observed fish swimming. They discussed and raised many questions such as how gills operate for fish to survive underwater. The natural environment provides a plethora of interest centres for pupils. Outside of the school setting, pupils notice interesting phenomenon such as why a mud puddle dried up, after a rain. Here, the pupil may learn about the water cycle such as moisture in the form of rain followed by needed factors for evaporation. Also, pupils may bring science objects to school for show and tell experiences which, for example, might well include tadpoles in a jar from a farm pond. These tadpoles will then be observed to notice the growth of feet and eventually become a mature frog. Excitement is in the air with pupil eagerness to tell about their show and tell objects (Blough and Schwartz (1984).

Fourth, a quality current events programme in science might well provide readiness for learning. In any newscast or news paper for children, there are a plethora of incidences which have just occurred. Thus, news items such as the following have occurred in different areas of the world;

- earthquakes, tornados, hurricanes
- mudslides, volcanic eruptions, gully and sheet erosion
- ice storms, floods, drought, hail, and strong wind gusts

Each of the above provide content for elaboration and discussions. Audio visual aids provide for clarity in current events presentations. Problem solving activities may occur through identifying a problem pertaining to the causes of each of the above, developing an hypothesis, evaluating the hypothesis, and making necessary modifications and revisions. Indepth learnings may then occur.

At the beginning of the primary school years, pupils already may develop conclusions in problem solving based on their individual maturity levels. All science teaching includes the following considerations :

- are the learnings on the understanding level of individual pupils?
- might pupils be motivated to realize high expectations?
- will the content be sequenced appropriately for optimal pupil progress?
- may indepth learning follow the readiness experiences? (Maheshwari, 2008).

Fifth, pupils need assistance to scaffold information. If, for example, a pupil did not attach meaning to the concept "reptiles", the science teacher may scaffold sequential activities to aid in its understanding. Depending upon the maturity level of the learner, the teacher might show pictures in the basal science textbook of snakes and turtles and briefly/clearly state why these are reptiles. The learner may verbalize, in return, what a reptile is to provide feedback to the teacher in revealing its understanding. With scaffolding, the pupil is able to learn more complicated subject matter than otherwise would be the case. Subject-matter chosen for scaffolding must be achievable, not beyond the capability of the pupil. The science teacher needs to receive feedback from the learner to notice if efforts at scaffolding have worked. If not, additional strategies need to be in the offing (Vygotsky, 1933,1978).

Sixth, metacognition must be stressed. Here, the pupil reflects upon what has/has not been learned. Thus, a pupil thinks about previous learnings to notice if readiness exists to acquire the ensuing subject matter. The science teacher, also, must reflect upon previously used teaching strategies to notice what worked and what did not work effectively. Modifications in teaching might then be made such as in the following :

- from the use of abstract learnings to emphasizing concrete experiences for pupils
- from rote learning to problem solving activities
- from lecture to inquiry learning
- from reading about science to doing science as in performing experiments, the heart of the science curriculum
- from being passive recipients of knowledge to actively pursuing tasks as in the project method
- from memorizing science subject matter to engaging in problem solving.

Seventh, learning styles (Searson and Dunn, 2001) have salient implications for teaching and learning. To provide readiness for learning, each pupil prefers a particular style more so than others. Thus, selected pupils may prefer cooperative learning rather than experiencing individual activities. The former have preferences to learn within a committee setting as compared to the latter who prefer to engage in learning opportunities by the self. For example in using the project method, a set of learners select to work together in developing a model volcano in an ongoing unit of study, whereas another pupil chooses to work on a model pertaining to folding and faulting individually. Further differences in styles of learning include the following :

- teacher guided instruction as compared to an open ended science curriculum
- a subject centred science curriculum instead of using pupil centered procedures

- the use of behaviorally stated objectives in instruction versus open ended objectives in teaching and learning situations
- a separate subjects science curriculum versus integrated units of study relating many academic disciplines.

The science teacher then must take into consideration under which conditions pupils learn best in ongoing lessons and units of study. Optimal pupil achievement is desired and therefore learning styles need consideration in choosing learning opportunities. Readiness for learning requires that science teachers take into consideration how pupils learn.

Eighth, readiness for learning must also take into consideration multiple intelligences theory. Thus, a pupil may possess one or more intelligences in the acquisition of knowledge and skills. Science has its own methods and subject matter. However, related content from other disciplines might assist pupils to achieve more optimally. The following intelligences may be brought in as needed to clarify and extend subject matter learnings :

- verbal as in reading and writing experiences
- logical as in reasoning about science phenomenon
- musical as in writing lyrics and putting them to music
- intrapersonal as in showing much strengths in working by the self
- interpersonal as in revealing much achievement in cooperative learning
- bodily/kinesthetic as in doing high quality projects and construction work
- scientific in thinking objectively in learnings dealing with the natural and social environment (See Gardner, 1993).

Ninth, portfolios might well assist the science teacher in determining pupil readiness for learning. Traditional or digital portfolios contain a representative sampling of pupil work in science lessons and units of study such as the following :

- book reports on science content
- photos of science projects and construction work, individually and/or committee endeavors
- samples of oral reading activities
- results from teacher written and standardized tests
- self evaluation in terms of recommended criteria
- art work products completed in science lessons and units of study
- creative written work as in writing poems and stories

By examining each of the above, the science teacher is better able to ascertain pupil readiness for learning as well as to assess pupil progress (Ediger, 2008-2009).

Tenth, a variety of evaluation procedures need to be used to ascertain learner achievement in science. These procedures must be valid and reliable, using the best criteria in the evaluation process when using :

- teacher written tests
- standardized and mandated tests
- teacher observation
- product and process evaluation.

REFERENCES

Blough, Glenn O., and Julius Schwartz (1984), *Elementary School Science and How To Teach It.* New York: Holt, Rinehart and Winston.

Ediger, Marlow (2007), *School Science Education.* New Delhi, India: Discovery Publishing House.

Ediger, Marlow (2008-2009) "Portfolios in Science," *Connecticut Journal of Science Education*, 47 (1), 28-29.

Gilbert, Jean, and Marleen Kotelman (2005), "Five Good Reasons to use Science Notebooks," *Science and Children*, 43 (3), 28-32.

Gardner, Howard (1993), *Multiple Intelligences: Theory Into Practice.* New York: Basic Books.

Maheshwari, Amrita (2008), "Integral Values of Science Education," *Edutracks*, 8 (4), 16-17.

National Research Council (1996), *National Science Education Standards.* Washington, DC: National Academy Press.

Searson, Robert and Rita Dunn (2001), "The Learning Styles Teaching Model," *Science and Children*, 38 (5), 22-36.

Vygotsky, L. S. (1933, 1978), *Mind in Society: The Development of Higher Psychological Processes.* Cambridge, Massachusetts: Harvard University Press.

Additional Reading

Amala, P.A. and Anupama, P., Authors and Digumarti Bhaskara Rao, Editor (2004). *History of Education.* New Delhi : Discovery Publishing House. ISBN 81-7141-860-0.

Appala Naidu, P.Ch., Author and Digumarti Bhaskara Rao, Editor (2007). *Student Feedback Methods.* New Delhi : Discovery Publishing House.

Bhaskara Rao, Digumarti (1994). *Scientific Aptitude.* New Delhi : Ashish Publishing House. ISBN 81-7024-658-X.

Bhaskara Rao, Digumarti (1995). *Animal Kingdom.* New Delhi : Discovery Publishing House. ISBN 81-7141-274-2.

Bhaskara Rao, Digumarti (1995). *Batracology.* New Delhi : Discovery Publishing House. ISBN 81-7141-279-3.

Bhaskara Rao, Digumarti (1997). *Scientific Attitude.* New Delhi : Discovery Publishing House. ISBN 81-7141-381-1.

Bhaskara Rao, Digumarti (1996). *Scientific Attitude vis-à-vis Scientific Aptitude.* New Delhi : Discovery Publishing House. ISBN 81-7141-308-0.

Bhaskara Rao, Digumarti (2004). *Scientific Attitude, Scientific Aptitude and Achievement.* New Delhi : Discovery Publishing House. ISBN 81-7141-781-7.

Bhaskara Rao, Digumarti (2004). *Educational Administration.* New Delhi : Discovery Publishing House. ISBN 81-7141-842-2.

Bhaskara Rao, Digumarti (2004). *Issues in School Education.* New Delhi : Discovery Publishing House. ISBN 81-8356-025-3.

Bhaskara Rao, Digumarti, Editor (1996). *Encyclopaedia of Education For All,* 5 Volumes. New Delhi : APH Publishing Corporation. ISBN 81-7024-759-4 (set).

Vol. I *Education For All : The World Conference.* ISBN 81-7024-760-8.

Vol. II *Education For All : The EPA-9 Summit.* ISBN 81-7024-761-6.

Vol. II *Education For All : Quality Education For All.* ISBN 81-7024-762-6.

Vol. IV *Education For All : Planning and Monitoring.* ISBN 81-7024-763-4.

Vol. V *Education For All : The Indian Scenario.* ISBN 81-7024-764-0.

Bhaskara Rao, Digumarti, Editor (1999). *International Encyclopaedia of AIDS,* 11 Volumes. New Delhi: Discovery Publishing House. ISBN 81-7141-522-6 (set).

Vol. 1 *Introduction to HIV/AIDS.* ISBN 81-7141-523-7.

Vol. 2 *HIV/AIDS – Issues and Challenges,* 2 parts. ISBN 81-7141-524-5.

Vol. 3 *HIV/AIDS – Socio Economic Realities.* ISBN 81-7141-524-3.

Vol. 4 *HIV/AIDS – Law Ethics and Human Rights,* 2 parts. ISBN 81-7141-526-1.

Vol. 5 *AIDS and NGOs.* ISBN 81-7141-527-X.

Vol. 6 *AIDS and Home Care.* ISBN 81-7141-528-8.

Vol. 7 *STD Case Management.* ISBN 81-7141-529-6.

Vol. 8 *HIV/AIDS Prevention and Care – Teaching Modules for Nurses and Midwives.* ISBN 81-7141-530-X.

Vol. 9 *HIV Prevention Education for Educational Institutions.* ISBN 81-7141-531-8.

Vol.10 *Instructional Modules for AIDS Education.* ISBN 81-7141-532-6.

Vol.11 *School Health Education to prevent AIDS and STD – A Package for Curriculum Planners.* ISBN 81-7141-533-4.

Bhaskara Rao, Digumarti, Editor (2000). *International Encyclopaedia of Human Rights,* 7 Volumes in 13 Parts. New Delhi : Discovery Publishing House. ISBN 81-7141-567-9 (set).

Vol. 1 *International Instruments of Human Rights,* 2 Parts. ISBN 81-7141-569-4.

Vol. 2 *Regional Instruments of Human Rights.* ISBN 81-7141-604-7.

Vol. 3 *Human Rights and the United Nations,* 2 parts. ISBN 81-7141-605-5.

Vol. 4 *Fact Files of Human Rights,* 3 Parts. ISBN 81-7141-606-3.

Vol. 5 *Study Stories of Human Rights,* 3 parts. ISBN 81-7141-607-3.

Vol. 6 *International Meetings on Human Rights,* 2 parts. ISBN 81-714-608-X.

Vol. 7 *Professional Training in Human Rights.* ISBN 81-7141-609-8.

Bhaskara Rao, Digumarti, Editor (2000). *International Encyclopaedia of Science and Technology Education*, 11 Volumes. New Delhi : Discovery Publishing House. ISBN 81-7141-548-2 (set).

Vol. 1 *Science and Technology Education.* ISBN 81-7141-568-7.

Vol. 2 *Science Education in Developing Countries.* ISBN 81-7141-569-9.

Vol. 3 *Organizational Structure of Science.* ISBN 81-7141-570-9.

Vol. 4 *Science Education in Asia and the Pacific.* ISBN 81-7141-571-7

Vol. 5 *Science and Technology Education For All.* ISBN 81-7141-572-5.

Vol. 6 *Values, Ethics, Talent and Girls in Science and Technology Education.* ISBN 81-7141-573-3.

Vol. 7 *Popularization of Science and Technology Education.* ISBN 81-7141-574-1.

Vol. 8 *Science, Power and Society.* ISBN 81-7141- 575-X.

Vol. 9 *Information Technology.* ISBN 81-7141-576-8.

Vol.10 *Teacher Training in Science and Technology Education.* ISBN 81-7142-577-6.

Vol.11 *Teacher Training in Science and Technology : A Curriculum Framework.* ISBN 81-7141-578-4.

Bhaskara Rao, Digumarti, Editor (2000). *Education For All : Achieving the Goal*, 3 Volumes. New Delhi : APH Publishing Corporation. ISBN 81-7648-152-1 (set).

Vol. I *The Global Consensus.* ISBN 81-7648-155-6.

Vol. II *Mid-Decade Review Reports of Regional Seminars.* ISBN 81-7648-154-8.

Vol. III *Issues and Trends.* ISBN 81-7648-155-6.

Bhaskara Rao, Digumarti, Editor (2004). *International Encyclopaedia of Learning to Live Together*, 4 Volumes. New Delhi : Discovery Publishing House. ISBN 81-7141-848-1.

Vol. 1 *International Conference on Learning to Live Together.*

Vol. 2 *Globalization and Living Together.*

Vol. 3 *Curriculum for Learning to Live Together.*

Vol. 4 *Science Education for the Contemporary Society .*

Bhaskara Rao, Digumarti, Editor (2005). *Encyclopaedia of Education For All*, 3 Volumes. New Delhi : Discovery Publishing House. ISBN 81-7141-647-0 (Set).

Bhaskara Rao, Digumarti, Editor (2007). *Encyclopaedia of Teacher Education*, 4 Volumes. New Delhi : Discovery Publishing House. ISBN 81-8356-306-6 (Set).

Bhaskara Rao, Digumarti, Editor (2007). *Encyclopaedia of Edeucation for Living Together*, 4 Volumes. New Delhi : Discovery Publishing House. ISBN 81-7141-848-1 (Set).

Bhaskara Rao, Digumarti, Editor (1996). *National Policy on Education*, 2 Volumes. New Delhi: Anmol Publications Pvt. Ltd. ISBN 81-7488-323-1.

Bhaskara Rao, Digumarti, Editor (1996). *Global Perceptions on Peace Education*, 3 Volumes. New Delhi : Discovery Publishing House. ISBN 81-7141-319-6.

Bhaskara Rao, Digumarti, Editor (1997). *Education for the 21st Century.* New Delhi : Discovery Publishing House. ISBN 81-7141-389-7.

Bhaskara Rao, Digumarti, Editor (1997). *Reflections on Scientific Attitude.* New Delhi : Discovery Publishing House. ISBN 81-7141-319-6.

Bhaskara Rao, Digumarti, Editor (1997). *Success Story of a Primary Education Project.* New Delhi : APH Publishing Corporation. ISBN 81-7024-850-7.

Bhaskara Rao, Digumarti, Editor (1997). *World Food Summit.* New Delhi : Discovery Publishing House. ISBN 81-7141-386-2.

Bhaskara Rao, Digumarti, Editor (1997). *Care the Child*, 2 Volumes. New Delhi: Discovery Publishing House. ISBN 81-7141-394-3.

Bhaskara Rao, Digumarti, Editor (1998). *Earth Summit*, 2 Volumes. New Delhi : Discovery Publishing House. ISBN 81-7141-435-4.

Bhaskara Rao, Digumarti, Editor (1998). *Adolescence Education.* New Delhi : Discovery Publishing House. ISBN 81-7141-432-X.

Bhaskara Rao, Digumarti, Editor (1998). *Community and School Nutrition Education.* New Delhi : Discovery Publishing House. ISBN 81-7141-435-4.

Bhaskara Rao, Digumarti, Editor (1998). *District Primary Education Programme.* New Delhi: Discovery Publishing House. ISBN 81-7141-396-X.

Bhaskara Rao, Digumarti, Editor (1998). *National Policy on Education : Towards an Enlightened and Humane Society.* New Delhi : Discovery Publishing House. ISBN 81-7141-426-5.

Bhaskara Rao, Digumarti, Editor (1998). *Reforming School Education.* New Delhi : Discovery Publishing House. ISBN 81-7141-403-6.

Bhaskara Rao, Digumarti, Editor (1998). *Teacher Education in India.* New Delhi : Discovery Publishing House. ISBN 81-7141-406-0.

Bhaskara Rao, Digumarti, Editor (1998). *World Summit for Social Development.* New Delhi : Discovery Publishing House. ISBN 81-7141-420-6.

Bhaskara Rao, Digumarti, Editor (2001). *Nuclear Materials : Issues and Concerns*, 2 Volumes. New Delhi : Discovery Publishing House. ISBN 81-7141-611-X.

Bhaskara Rao, Digumarti, Editor (2001). *Distance Education in Different Countries.* New Delhi : APH Publishing Corporation. ISBN 81-7648-229-3.

Bhaskara Rao, Digumarti, Editor (2001). *Decentralised Management of Education : Management of Education in Panchayati Raj and Municipal Bodies.* New Delhi : Discovery Publishing House. ISBN 81-7141-617-9.

Bhaskara Rao, Digumarti, Editor (2001). *Electrochemistry for Environmental Protection.* New Delhi: Discovery Publishing House. ISBN 81-7141-619-5.

Bhaskara Rao, Digumarti, Editor (2001). *Global Educational Studies.* New Delhi : Discovery Publishing House. ISBN 81-7141-616-0.

Bhaskara Rao, Digumarti, Editor (2001). *Global Synthesis of Educational Assessment.* New Delhi : Discovery Publishing House. ISBN 81-7141-613-6.

Bhaskara Rao, Digumarti, Editor (2001). *Jomtein Decade of Education.* New Delhi : Discovery Publishing House. ISBN 81-7141-618-7.

Bhaskara Rao, Digumarti, Editor (2001). *World Conference on Education for All.* New Delhi: APH Publishing Corporation. ISBN 81-7141-274-9.

Bhaskara Rao, Digumarti, Editor (2001). *World Conference on Higher Education.* New Delhi : Discovery Publishing House. ISBN 81-7141-610-1.

Bhaskara Rao, Digumarti, Editor (2001). *World Conference on Science.* New Delhi : Discovery Publishing House. ISBN 81-7141-612-8.

Bhaskara Rao, Digumarti, Editor (2003). *Inspiring Experiences in Teacher Education.* New Delhi : Discovery Publishing House. ISBN 81-7141-656-X.

Bhaskara Rao, Digumarti, Editor (2003). *International Studies in Education*, 3 Volumes. New Delhi : Discovery Publishing House. ISBN 81-7141-647-0.

Bhaskara Rao, Digumarti, Editor (2003). *Military Conversion : Impact on Science and Technology.* New Delhi : Discovery Publishing House. ISBN 81-7141-578-4.

Bhaskara Rao, Digumarti, Editor (2003). *United Nations Millennium Summit.* New Delhi : Discovery Publishing House. ISBN 81-7141-632-2.

Bhaskara Rao, Digumarti, Editor (2003). *World Assembly on Aging.* New Delhi : Discovery Publishing House. ISBN 81-7141-637-3.

Bhaskara Rao, Digumarti, Editor (2003). *World Conference on Human Rights.* New Delhi: Discovery Publishing House. ISBN 81-7141-661-6.

Bhaskara Rao, Digumarti, Editor (2003). *World Education Forum.* New Delhi: Discovery Publishing House. ISBN 81-7141-639-X.

Bhaskara Rao, Digumarti, Editor (2003). *Education, Employment and Human Resource Development.* New Delhi : Discovery Publishing House. ISBN 81-7141- 681-0.

Bhaskara Rao, Digumarti, Editor (2003). *Successful Schooling.* New Delhi : Discovery Publishing House. ISBN 81-7141-677-2.

Bhaskara Rao, Digumarti, Editor (2003). *European Education and Teachers.* New Delhi: Discovery Publishing House. ISBN 81-7141-702-7.

Bhaskara Rao, Digumarti, Editor (2003). *Teachers in a Changing World.* New Delhi : Discovery Publishing House. ISBN 81-7141-694-2.

Bhaskara Rao, Digumarti, Editor (2004). *International Guidelines on Open and Distance Teacher Education.* New Delhi: Discovery Publishing House. ISBN 81-7141-777-9.

Bhaskara Rao, Digumarti, Editor (2004). *Adult Learning in the 21st Century.* New Delhi: Discovery Publishing House. ISBN 81-7141-797-3.

Bhaskara Rao, Digumarti, Editor (2004). *Educational Practices : Research and Recommendations.* New Delhi: Discovery Publishing House. ISBN 81-7141-835-X.

Bhaskara Rao, Digumarti, Editor (2004). *General Secondary Education In the 21st Century.* New Delhi: Discovery Publishing House.

Bhaskara Rao, Digumarti, Editor (2004). *Reforming Secondary Education.* New Delhi: Discovery Publishing House. ISBN 81-7141-843-0.

Bhaskara Rao, Digumarti, Editor (2004). *Human Rights Education.* New Delhi : Discovery Publishing House. ISBN 81-7141-882-1.

Bhaskara Rao, Digumarti, Editor (2004). *United Nations Decade for Human Rights Education.* New Delhi : Discovery Publishing House. ISBN 81-7141- 887-2.

Bhaskara Rao, Digumarti, Editor (2004). *Technical and Vocational Education and Training in the 21st Century.* New Delhi : Discovery Publishing House. ISBN 81-7141-984-4.

Bhaskara Rao, Digumarti, Editor (2005). *Encyclopaedia of Education For All,* 5 Volumes. New Delhi : Discovery Publishing House.

Bhaskara Rao, Digumarti and B.S.V. Dutt, Editors (2003). *Education : Programmes and Policies.* New Delhi : APH Publishing Corporation. ISBN 81-7648-470-9.

Bhaskara Rao, Digumarti, C.A.P. Swamy and B.S.V. Dutt (1997). *Self-Evaluation in Student Teaching.* New Delhi : Discovery Publishing House. ISBN 81-7141-374-9.

Bhaskara Rao, Digumarti and C.D. Swarna Lattha, Editors (2006). *Encyclopaedia of Biotechnology*, 5 Volumes. New Delhi : Discovery Publishing House. ISBN 81-8356-168-3 (set).

Bhaskara Rao, Digumarti, C. Sridevi and K. Vijaya (1995). *Achievement in Social Studies.* New Delhi: Discovery Publishing House. ISBN 81-7141-281-5.

Bhaskara Rao, Digumarti and D. Naresh Kumar (2004). *School Teacher Effectiveness.* New Delhi : Discovery Publishing House. ISBN 81-7141-782-5.

Bhaskara Rao, Digumarti and D. Sridhar (2002). *Job Satisfaction of School Teachers.* New Delhi : Discovery Publishing House. ISBN 81-7141-652-7.

Bhaskara Rao, Digumarti and Digumarti Pushpa Latha, Editors (1998). *International Encyclopaedia of Women*, 5 Volumes. New Delhi : Discovery Publishing House. ISBN 81-7141-410-9 (Set).

Vol. 1 *Status of World's Women*. ISBN 81-7141- 494-X.

Vol. 2 *Women, Education and Empowerment.* ISBN 81-7141-498-1.

Vol. 3 *Women Challenges and Advancement*. ISBN 81-7141-497-4.

Vol. 4 *Women and Family Health*. ISBN 81-7141- 497-4.

Vol. 5 *Women and International Action*. ISBN 81-7141-498-2.

Babu, P.C., Author and Digumarti Bhaskara Rao, Editor (2004). *Flowers of Wisdom.* New Delhi : Discovery Publishing House. ISBN 81-7141-695-0.

Babu, P.C., Author and Digumarti Bhaskara Rao, Editor (2008). *Worlds of Wisdom.* New Delhi: Discovery Publishing House.

Bhagya Lakshmi, L., Author and Digumarti Bhaskara Rao, Editor (2000). *Reading and Comprehension.* New Delhi : Discovery Publishing House. ISBN 81-7141-543-1.

Bhasha, S.A., Author and Digumarti Bhaskara Rao, Editor (2004). *Methods of Teaching Geography.* New Delhi : Discovery Publishing House. ISBN 81-7141-807-4.

Bhaskara Rao, Digumarti (1986). *Dhrushya Sravana Bodhanapakaranalu* (Audio Visual Teaching Aids). Guntur : Nagarjuna Publishers.

Bhaskara Rao, Digumarti (1993). *Jeevasashtra Bodhana* (Teaching of Biology). Guntur : Nagarjuna Publishers.

Bhaskara Rao, Digumarti (1994). *Vidya Manovignana Sastram* (Educational Psychology). Guntur : Nagarjuna Publishers.

Bhaskara Rao, Digumarti (1995). *Vignanasasthra Bodhana* (Teaching of science) Guntur : Nagarjuna Publishers.

Bhaskara Rao, Digumarti (1997). *Vidya Manovignana Sastram* (Educational Psychology). Guntur : Creative Press.

Bhaskara Rao, Digumarti (1998). *DSC Study Material.* Guntur : Nagarjuna Publishers.

Bhaskara Rao, Digumarti (1998). *Upadhyayudu Vidya.* (Teacher and Education) Guntur : Nagarjuna Publishers.

Bhaskara Rao, Digumarti (1998). *Vidya Drukpadalu* (Perspectives of Education). Guntur : Nagarjuna Publishers.

Bhaskara Rao, Digumarti (1999). *EdCET Teaching Aptitude.* Guntur : Nagarjuna Publishers.

Bhaskara Rao, Digumarti (2001). *Bharata Samajamulo Upadyayudu Vidhya* (Teacher and Education in Emerging Indian Society). Guntur : Sri Nagarjuna Publishers.

Bhaskara Rao, Digumarti (2001). *Bhoutika Sastra Bodhana Padhatulu* (Methods of Teaching Physical Science). Guntur : Sri Nagarjuna Publishers.

Bhaskara Rao, Digumarti (2001). *Jeeva Sastra Bodhana Padhatulu* (Methods of Teaching Biology). Guntur : Sri Nagarjuna Publishers.

Bhaskara Rao, Digumarti (2001). *Vidya Manovignana Sastram* (Educational Psychology). Guntur : Sri Nagarjuna Publishers.

Bhaskara Rao, Digumarti (2003). *Patasala Yajamanyam / Paripalana* (School Management and Administration). Guntur : Sri Nagarjuna Publishers.

Bhaskara Rao, Digumarti and A. Jagadish (2009). *Vignansastra Bodhana Padhatulu* (Methods of Teaching Science).Guntur : Sri Nagarjuna Publishers.

Bhaskara Rao, Digumarti and B. Prasad Babu (2009). *Pradhamika Vidya mariyu Vileena Vidya Dhrukpadhalu* (Perspectives in Primary Education and Inclusive Education). Guntur : Sri Nagarjuna Publishers.

Bhaskara Rao, Digumarti and B. Prasad Babu (2009). *Vidya Manovignana Sastram* (Educational Psychology). Guntur : Sri Nagarjuna Publishers.

Bhaskara Rao, Digumarti and D. Naresh Kumar (2004). *School Teacher Effectiveness.* New Delhi : Discovery Publishing House. ISBN 81-7141-782-5.

Bhaskara Rao, Digumarti and Digumarthi Harshitha (2004). *Adjustment of Adolescents.* New Delhi: APH Publishing House. ISBN 81-7648-836-8.

Bhaskara Rao, Digumarti and Digumarthi Harshitha, Editors (2001). *Education in India.* New Delhi: APH Publishing House. ISBN 81-7648-207-2.

Bhaskara Rao, Digumarti and Digumarti Pushpa Latha (1994). *Achievement in Biology.* New Delhi : Discovery Publishing House. ISBN 81-7141-264-5.

Bhaskara Rao, Digumarti and Digumarti Pushpa Latha (1994). *Achievement in Science.* New Delhi : Discovery Publishing House. ISBN 81-7141-280-70.

Bhaskara Rao, Digumarti and Digumarti Pushpa Latha (1995). *Achievement in English.* New Delhi : Discovery Publishing House. ISBN 81-7141-283-1.

Bhaskara Rao, Digumarti and Digumarti Pushpa Latha (1995). *Achievement in Mathematics.* New Delhi : Discovery Publishing House. ISBN 81-7141-278-5.

Bhaskara Rao, Digumarti and Digumarti Pushpa Latha (2004). *Education for Women.* New Delhi : Discovery Publishing House. ISBN 81-7141-873-2.

Bhaskara Rao, Digumarti and E. Sreekanth Babu (2004). *Educational Interests of School Students.* New Delhi : Discovery Publishing House. ISBN 81-7141-837-6.

Bhaskara Rao, Digumarti and G. Prasanthi (2009). *Samardya Nirmanamu* (Capacity Building). Guntur : Sri Nagarjuna Publishers.

Bhaskara Rao, Digumarti and K. Subba Rao (2009). *Elementary Vidya, Pranalika, Yajamanyam, Upadyaya Kartavyalu* (Elementary Education, Planning, Management and Teacher Functions). Guntur : Sri Nagarjuna Publishers.

Bhaskara Rao, Digumarti and K. Vijaya (1995). *A Text Book Evaluation.* Ambala Cantt : The Associated Publishers.

Bhaskara Rao, Digumarti and K.R.S. Sambasiva Rao, Editors (1996). *Current Trends in Indian Education.* New Delhi : Discovery Publishing House. ISBN 81-7141-311-0.

Bhaskara Rao, Digumarti and M.A. Fayaz (2004). *Problems of Primary School Drop-outs.* New Delhi : Discovery Publishing House. ISBN 81-7141- 834-1.

Bhaskara Rao, Digumarti and N.V.M. Mohana Rao (2002). *Problems of Mentally Handicapped Children.* New Delhi : Discovery Publishing House. ISBN 81-7141- 645-4.

Bhaskara Rao, Digumarti and S. Chandra Mohan (2002). *Sports Management.* New Delhi : APH Publishing House. ISBN 81-7648-467-9.

Bhaskara Rao, Digumarti and S.A. Khader (2004). *Problems of Private School Teachers.* New Delhi : Discovery Publishing Corporation. ISBN 81-7141-838-4.

Bhaskara Rao, Digumarti and S.A. Khader (2004). *School Education in India.* New Delhi : Discovery Publishing Corporation. ISBN 81-7141-849-X.

Bhaskara Rao, Digumarti and Sk. Johni Basha (2004). *Teachers' Population Education Awareness.* New Delhi : Discovery Publishing House. ISBN 81-7141-832-5.

Bhaskara Rao, Digumarti, Digumarthi Harshitha and K.R.S. Sambasiva Rao, Editors (1999). *Advanced Biotechnology.* New Delhi : Discovery Publishing House. ISBN 81-7141-516-4.

Bhaskara Rao, Digumarti, Digumarti Pushpa Latha and Digumarthi Harshitha, Editors (2001). *Biological Warfare.* New Delhi: Discovery Publishing House. ISBN 81-7141-597-0.

Bhaskara Rao, Digumarti, Digumarti Pushpa Latha and Digumarthi Harshitha, Editors (2001). *Women as Educators.* New Delhi: Discovery Publishing House. ISBN 81-7141-602-0.

Bhaskara Rao, Digumarti, Digumarti Pushpa Latha and Digumarthi Harshitha, Editors (2001). *Assessing Learning Achievement.* New Delhi: Discovery Publishing House. ISBN 81-7141-601-2.

Bhaskara Rao, Digumarti, Digumarti Pushpa Latha and Digumarthi Harshitha, Editors (2001). *Energy Security.* New Delhi : Discovery Publishing House. ISBN 81-7141-598-9.

Bhaskara Rao, Digumarti, Editor (2010). *Elementary Vidya, Pranalika, Yajamanyam, Upadyaya Kartavyalu – Question Bank* (Elementary Education, Planning, Management and Teacher Functions). Guntur: Sri Nagarjuna Publishers.

Bhaskara Rao, Digumarti, Editor (2010). *Ganithasastra Bodhana Padhatulu – Question Bank* (Methods of Teaching Science).Guntur : Sri Nagarjuna Publishers.

Bhaskara Rao, Digumarti, Editor (2010). *Methods of Teaching English – Question Bank.* Guntur : Sri Nagarjuna Publishers.

Bhaskara Rao, Digumarti, Editor (2010). *Pradhamika Vidya mariyu Vileena Vidya Dhrukpadhalu – Question Bank* (Perspectives in Primary Education and Inclusive Education). Guntur : Sri Nagarjuna Publishers.

Bhaskara Rao, Digumarti, Editor (2010). *Samardya Nirmanamu – Question Bank* (Capacity Building). Guntur : Sri Nagarjuna Publishers.

Bhaskara Rao, Digumarti, Editor (2010). *Sanghikasastra Bodhana Padhatulu – Question Bank* (Methods of Teaching Social Studies).Guntur : Sri Nagarjuna Publishers.

Bhaskara Rao, Digumarti, Editor (2010). *Telugu Bodhana Padhatulu – Question Bank* (Methods of Teaching Social Studies).Guntur: Sri Nagarjuna Publishers.

Bhaskara Rao, Digumarti, Editor (2010). *Vidya Manovignana Sastram – Question Bank* (Educational Psychology). Guntur : Sri Nagarjuna Publishers.

Bhaskara Rao, Digumarti, Editor (2010). *Vignansastra Bodhana Padhatulu – Question Bank* (Methods of Teaching Science).Guntur : Sri Nagarjuna Publishers.

Bhaskara Rao, Digumarti, N. Saraja, J. Lalitha and V. Mrunalini, Translators (2008). *Vidya – Samajam (Education - Society). Hyderabad* : Dr. B.R. Ambedkar Open University.

Bhaskara Rao, Digumarti, V.V. Rao, V.V. Lakshmi and V.V. Krishna, Editors (1999). *Status and Advancement of Women.* New Delhi: APH Publishing Corporation. ISBN 81-7648-169-6.

Bhuvaneswara Lakshmi, G. and K. Subba Rao, Authors and Digumarti Bhaskara Rao, Editor (2004). *Methods of Teaching Biology.* New Delhi : Discovery Publishing House. ISBN 81-7141-914-3.

Bhuvaneswara Lakshmi, G., Author and Digumarti Bhaskara Rao, Editor (2004). *Methods of Teaching Life Science.* New Delhi : Discovery Publishing House. ISBN 81-7141-804-X.

Bhuvaneswara Lakshmi, Gadde, Author and Digumarti Bhaskara Rao, Editor(2000). *Attitude Towards Science.* New Delhi: Discovery Publishing House. ISBN 81-7141-541-6.

Bujji Babu, K., Author and Digumarti Bhaskara Rao, Editor (2007). *Teaching Aptitude of Primary School Teachers.* New Delhi: Sonali Publications. ISBN 81-8411-083-9.

Chary, K.V.N.B., Author and Digumarti Bhaskara Rao, Editor (2006). *Techniques of Teaching Physics.* New Delhi : Sonali Publications. ISBN 81-8411-046-4.

Chowdary, S.B.J.R. and Naga Raju, Authors and Digumarti Bhaskara Rao, Editor (2004). *Mastery of Teaching Skills.* New Delhi : Discovery Publishing House. ISBN 81-7141-861-9.

Dayakara Reddy, V. and Digumarti Bhaskara Rao, Editors (2006). *Value-Oriented Education.* New Delhi : Discovery Publishing House. ISBN 81-8356-051-2.

Devraj, T.A.S., Author and Digumarti Bhaskara Rao, Editor (1997). *Trace Analysis of Uranium and Thorium.* New Delhi : Discovery Publishing House. ISBN 81-7141-375-7.

Digumarti Bhaskara Rao and M. Srihari (2009). *Vardamana Bharata Desamulo Vidya* (Education in Emerging India). Guntur : Sri Nagarjuna Publishers.

Digumarti Bhaskara Rao, Editor (2010). *Vardamana Bharata Desamulo Vidya – Question Bank* (Education in Emerging India). Guntur : Sri Nagarjuna Publishers.

Durga Rani, K., Author and Digumarti Bhaskara Rao, Editor (2000). *Educational Aspirations and Scientific Attitudes.* New Delhi : Discovery Publishing House. ISBN 81-7141-555-5.

Dutt, B.S.V. and Digumarti Bhaskara Rao (2001). *Empowering Primary Teachers.* New Delhi : Discovery Publishing House. ISBN 81-7141-615-2.

Dutt, B.S.V., Author and Digumarti Bhaskara Rao, Editor (2004). *Comparative Education.* New Delhi: Discovery Publishing House. ISBN 81-7141-912-7.

Ediger, Marlow and Digumarti Bhaskara Rao (1996). *Science Curriculum.* New Delhi: Discovery Publishing House. ISBN 81-7141-321-8.

Ediger, Marlow and Digumarti Bhaskara Rao (2000). *Teaching Mathematics Successfully.* New Delhi : Discovery Publishing House. ISBN 81-7141-552-0.

Ediger, Marlow and Digumarti Bhaskara Rao (2001). *Teaching Science Successfully.* New Delhi : Discovery Publishing House. ISBN 81-7141-600-4.

Ediger, Marlow and Digumarti Bhaskara Rao (2001). *Teaching Social Studies Successfully.* New Delhi : Discovery Publishing House. ISBN 81-7141-596-2.

Ediger, Marlow and Digumarti Bhaskara Rao (2002). *Elementary Curriculum.* New Delhi : Discovery Publishing House. ISBN 81-7141-658-6.

Ediger, Marlow and Digumarti Bhaskara Rao (2002). *Improving School Administration.* New Delhi : Discovery Publishing House. ISBN 81-7141-633-0

Ediger, Marlow and Digumarti Bhaskara Rao (2002). *Philosophy and Curriculum.* New Delhi: Discovery Publishing House. ISBN 81-7141-631-4.

Ediger, Marlow and Digumarti Bhaskara Rao (2003). *Elementary Curriculum Improvement.* New Delhi : Discovery Publishing House. ISBN 81-7141-740-X.

Ediger, Marlow and Digumarti Bhaskara Rao (2003). *Language Arts Curriculum.* New Delhi : Discovery Publishing House. ISBN 81-7141-657-8.

Ediger, Marlow and Digumarti Bhaskara Rao (2003). *Psychology and Curriculum.* New Delhi : Discovery Publishing House. ISBN 81-7141-691-8.

Ediger, Marlow and Digumarti Bhaskara Rao (2003). *School Curriculum and Administration.* New Delhi : Discovery Publishing House. ISBN 81-7141-709-4.

Ediger, Marlow and Digumarti Bhaskara Rao (2003). *School Curriculum and Administration.* New Delhi : Discovery Publishing House. ISBN 81-7141-709-4.

Ediger, Marlow and Digumarti Bhaskara Rao (2003). *Teaching Language Arts Successfully.* New Delhi : Discovery Publishing House. ISBN 81-7141-678-0.

Ediger, Marlow and Digumarti Bhaskara Rao (2003). *Teaching Mathematics in Elementary Schools.* New Delhi : Discovery Publishing House. ISBN 81-7141-687-X.

Ediger, Marlow and Digumarti Bhaskara Rao (2003). *Teaching Science in Elementary Schools.* New Delhi: Discovery Publishing House. ISBN 81-7141-698-5.

Ediger, Marlow and Digumarti Bhaskara Rao (2004). *Relevancy in Elementary Curriculum.* New Delhi : Discovery Publishing House. ISBN 81-7141-845-9.

Ediger, Marlow and Digumarti Bhaskara Rao (2004). *School Organisation.* New Delhi : Discovery Publishing House. ISBN 81-7141-843-0.

Ediger, Marlow and Digumarti Bhaskara Rao (2005). *Quality School Education.* New Delhi : Discovery Publishing House. ISBN 81-8356-022-9.

Ediger, Marlow and Digumarti Bhaskara Rao (2006). *Administration of Schools.* New Delhi : Discovery Publishing House.

Ediger, Marlow and Digumarti Bhaskara Rao (2006). *Community College – Curriculum and Teaching.* New Delhi : Discovery Publishing House. ISBN 81-8356-053-9.

Ediger, Marlow and Digumarti Bhaskara Rao (2006). *Curriculum of School Subjects.* New Delhi : Discovery Publishing House.

Ediger, Marlow and Digumarti Bhaskara Rao (2006). *Curriculum Organisation.* New Delhi: Discovery Publishing House.

Ediger, Marlow and Digumarti Bhaskara Rao (2006). *Issues in School Curruculum.* New Delhi : Discovery Publishing House. ISBN 81-8356-052-0.

Ediger, Marlow and Digumarti Bhaskara Rao (2006). *Reading Curriculum and Instruction.* New Delhi : Discovery Publishing House.

Ediger, Marlow and Digumarti Bhaskara Rao (2006). *Successful School Education.* New Delhi : Discovery Publishing House. ISBN 81-8356-054-7.

Ediger, Marlow and Digumarti Bhaskara Rao (2006). *Successful School Administration.* New Delhi : Discovery Publishing House. ISBN 81-8356-046-6.

Ediger, Marlow and Digumarti Bhaskara Rao (2007). *Language Arts Education.* New Delhi : Discovery Publishing House. ISBN 81-8356-333-3.

Ediger, Marlow and Digumarti Bhaskara Rao (2007). *School Science Education.* New Delhi : Discovery Publishing House. ISBN 81-8356-352-X.

Ediger, Marlow and Digumarti Bhaskara Rao (2010). *Effective Schooling.* New Delhi : Discovery Publishing House. ISBN 978-81-8356-613-1.

Ediger, Marlow and Digumarti Bhaskara Rao (2010). *Effective School Curriculum.* New Delhi : Discovery Publishing House. ISBN 978-81-8356-585-1.

Ediger, Marlow and Digumarti Bhaskara Rao (2010). *Essays on Teaching Science.* New Delhi : Discovery Publishing House.

Ediger, Marlow and Digumarti Bhaskara Rao (2010). *Essays on Teaching Social Studies.* New Delhi : Discovery Publishing House.

Ediger, Marlow and Digumarti Bhaskara Rao (2010). *Essays on Teaching Reading.* New Delhi : Discovery Publishing House.

Ediger, Marlow and Digumarti Bhaskara Rao (2010). *Essays on Teaching Mathematics.* New Delhi : Discovery Publishing House.

Ediger, Marlow and Digumarti Bhaskara Rao (2010). *Essays on Teaching and Learning.* New Delhi : Discovery Publishing House.

Ediger, Marlow and Digumarti Bhaskara Rao, Editors (2006). *Encyclopaedia of School Education*, 5 Volumes. New Delhi : Discovery Publishing House. ISBN 81-8356-308-2 (set).

Ediger, Marlow and Digumarti Bhaskara Rao, Editors (2006). *Encyclopaedia of School Administration*, 4 Volumes. New Delhi : Discovery Publishing House. ISBN 81-8356-307-4 (set).

Ediger, Marlow and Digumarti Bhaskara Rao, Editors (2007). *Encyclopaedia of School Curriculum*, 10 Volumes. New Delhi : Discovery Publishing House. ISBN 81-8356-305-8 (set).

Ediger, Marlow and Digumarti Bhaskara Rao, Editors (2007). *Encyclopaedia of Teaching*, 8 Volumes. New Delhi : Discovery Publishing House. ISBN 81-8356-305-8 (set).

Ediger, Marlow, B.S.V. Dutt and Digumarti Bhaskara Rao (2003). *Teaching English Successfully.* New Delhi : Discovery Publishing House. ISBN 81-7141-707-8.

Elizabeth, M.E.S., Author and Digumarti Bhaskara Rao, Editor (2004). *Methods of Teaching English.* New Delhi : Discovery Publishing House. ISBN 81-7141-809-0.

Elizabeth, M.E.S., Author and Digumarti Bhaskara Rao, Editor (2004). *Acquisition of English Vocabulary.* New Delhi : Discovery Publishing House. ISBN 81-8356-075-X.

Fatima, Sk. and Digumarti Bhaskara Rao (2008). *Reasoning Ability of Adolescent Students.* New Delhi : Sonali Publications.

Fatima, Sk. Author and Digumarti Bhaskara Rao, Editor (2007). *Reasoning Ability of School Students.* New Delhi : Discovery Publishing House. ISBN 81-8356-330-9.

G.E.P. Sastry and G. Satya Narayana, Authors, Bhaskara Rao, Digumarti, Editor (2009). *Sanghikasastra Bodhana Padhatulu* (Methods of Teaching Social Studies).Guntur : Sri Nagarjuna Publishers.

Gopala Krishna, G., A. Rama Krishna, K. Subba Rao and Bhaskara Rao, Digumarti (2004). *Jeevasashtra Bodhana Padhatulu* (Methods of Teaching of Biological science). Guntur : Sri Nagarjuna Publishers.

Gopala Krishna, M., Author and Digumarti Bhaskara Rao, Editor (2007). *Techniques of Teaching Physical Education.* New Delhi : Sonali Publications. ISBN 81-8411-044-8.

Gopala Krishna, M., Author and Digumarti Bhaskara Rao, Editor (2007). *Techniques of Teaching Education.* New Delhi : Sonali Publications. ISBN 81-8411-062-6.

Harshitha, Digumarthi, Author and Digumarti Bhaskara Rao, Editor (2004). *Methods of Teaching Information Technology.* New Delhi : Discovery Publishing House. ISBN 81-7141-805-8.

Harshitha, Digumarthi, Author and Digumarti Bhaskara Rao, Editor (2007). *Techniques of Teaching Computer Science.* New Delhi : Sonali Publications. ISBN 81-8411-036-7.

Indira Devi, Author and J. Prasanth Kumar and Digumarti Bhaskara Rao, Editors (2004). *Values in Language Text Books.* New Delhi : Discovery Publishing House. ISBN 81-7141-833-3.

Jalaja Kumari, C., Author and Digumarti Bhaskara Rao, Editor (2004). *Methods of Teaching Educational Technology.* New Delhi : Discovery Publishing House. ISBN 81-7141-810-4.

Jalaja Kumari, C., Author and Digumarti Bhaskara Rao, Editor (2007). *Job Satisfaction of Teachers.* New Delhi : Discovery Publishing House.

Janardhan Reddy, B., Author and Digumarti Bhaskara Rao, Editor (2006). *Techniques of Teaching Sociology.* New Delhi : Sonali Publications. ISBN 81-8411-042-1.

Jayasree, K., Author and Digumarti Bhaskara Rao, Editor (1999). *Correlates of Socialisation.* New Delhi : Discovery Publishing House. ISBN 81-7141-517-2.

Jayasree, K., Author and Digumarti Bhaskara Rao, Editor (2004). *Methods of Teaching Science.* New Delhi : Discovery Publishing House. ISBN 81-7141-801-5.

John Babu, C., Author and T.J.R. Prasad, G.M. Madhukar and Digumarti Bhaskara Rao, Editors (2004). *Problem Solving in Mathematics.* New Delhi : APH Publishing Corporation. ISBN 81-7648-273-0.

Joseph Raju, B and G.A. Anitha, Authors and Digumarti Bhaskara Rao, Editor (2004). *Population Education.* New Delhi : Sonali Publications. ISBN 81-88836-31-3.

Krishna Murthy, V., K.S. Sudheer Reddy and Digumarti Bhaskara Rao (2004). *Vidya Manovignana Sastra Adharalu* (Foundations of Educational Psychology). Guntur : Sri Nagarjuna Publishers.

Krishna, G., Author and Digumarti Bhaskara Rao, Editor (2006). *Techniques of Teaching Physical Education.* New Delhi : Discovery Publishing House. ISBN 81-8411-044-8.

Kumar Raja, G., Author and Digumarti Bhaskara Rao, Editor (2007). *Principles of Primary School.* New Delhi : Sonali Publications. ISBN 81-8411-054-5.

Lakshmi Kumari, V., Author and Digumarti Bhaskara Rao, Editor (2006). *Techniques of Teaching Home Science.* New Delhi : Discovery Publishing House. ISBN 81-8411-048-0.

Lalini, V., V. Dayakara Reddy, M. Srihari and Digumarti Bhaskara Rao (2004). *Vidya Adharalu* (Foundations of Education). Guntur : Sri Nagarjuna Publishers.

Lalitha, T., Author and K.S. Prabhakaram, D.S.N. Sastry and Digumarti Bhaskara Rao, Editors (2004). *Educational Philosophic Beliefs.* New Delhi: Discovery Publishing House. ISBN 81-7141-765-5.

Madhava, K., Author and Digumarti Bhaskara Rao, Editor (2008). *Personality of Adolescent Students.* New Delhi: Sonali Publications.

Madhu Bala, Jampala, Author and Digumarti Bhaskara Rao, Editor (2004). *Methods of Teaching Exceptional Children.* New Delhi: Discovery Publishing House. ISBN 81-7141-802-3.

Madhu Bala, Jampala, Author and Digumarti Bhaskara Rao, Editor (2007). *Adjustment, Achievement Motivation and Academic Achievement of Hearing Impaired Students.* New Delhi: Discovery Publishing House

Marja, Talvi and Digumarti Bhaskara Rao, Editors (1996). *Educational Leadership and Social Changes.* New Delhi : Discovery Publishing House. ISBN 81-7141-320-X.

Marlow Ediger and Digumarti Bhaskara Rao, Editors (2006). *Encyclopaedia of School Education*, 5 Volumes. New Delhi : Discovery Publishing House. ISBN 81-8356-308-2 (Set).

Marlow Ediger and Digumarti Bhaskara Rao, Editors (2006). *Encyclopaedia of School Administration*, 4 Volumes. New Delhi : Discovery Publishing House. ISBN 81-8356-307-4 (set).

Marlow Ediger and Digumarti Bhaskara Rao, Editors (2007). *Encyclopaedia of School Curriculum*, 10 Volumes. New Delhi : Discovery Publishing House. ISBN 81-8356-305-8 (set).

Marlow Ediger and Digumarti Bhaskara Rao, Editors (2007). *Encyclopaedia of Teaching*, 8 Volumes. New Delhi : Discovery Publishing House. ISBN 81-8356-305-8 (set).

Naga Kumari, U., Author and Digumarti Bhaskara Rao, Editor (2008). *Science Process Skills of School Students*. New Delhi : Sonali Publications.

Nageswara Rao, S. and M. Srihari, Authors and Digumarti Bhaskara Rao, Editor (2004). *Guidance and Counselling*. New Delhi : Discovery Publishing House. ISBN 81-7141-840-6.

Nageswara Rao, S. and P. Sridhar, Authors and Digumarti Bhaskara Rao, Editor (2004). *Methods and Techniques of Teaching*. New Delhi : Sonali Publications. ISBN 81-88836-33-8.

Nageswara Rao, S., Author and Digumarti Bhaskara Rao, Editor (2006). *Techniques of Teaching Psychology*. New Delhi : Discovery Publishing House. ISBN 81-8411-040-5.

Nirmala Jyothi, M., Author and Digumarti Bhaskara Rao, Editor (2003). *Non-detention System in School Education*. New Delhi : Discovery Publishing House. ISBN 81-7141-654-3.

Padma Tulasi, G., Author and Digumarti Bhaskara Rao, Editor (2004). *Methods of Teaching Elementary Science*. New Delhi : Discovery Publishing House. ISBN 81-7141-871-6.

Pala Prasada Rao, V., Author and D. Bhaskara Rao, Editors (2008). *Functioning of Autonomous Colleges*. New Delhi : Sonali Publications.

Pala Prasada Rao, V., Author and K. N. Rani and D. Bhaskara Rao, Editors (2004).*India Pakistan : Partition Perspectives in Indo English Novels*. New Delhi: Discovery Publishing House. ISBN 81-7141-871-6.

Pitchi Reddy, M., Author and Digumarti Bhaskara Rao, Editor (2007). *Techniques of Teaching Social Sciences*. New Delhi : Sonali Publications. ISBN 81-8411-066-X.

Prabhakaram, K.S., Author and Digumarti Bhaskara Rao, Editors (1998). *Concept Attainment Model in Mathematics Teaching*. New Delhi : Discovery Publishing House. ISBN 81-7141-424-9.

Prasad Babu, B., Author and M.V.R. Raju and Digumarti Bhaskara Rao, Editors (2006). *Behavioural Problems of School Children*. New Delhi: Discovery Publishing House. ISBN 81-8356-206-X.

Prasad Babu, B., Author and P. Madhu and Digumarti Bhaskara Rao, Editors (2006). *Psychological Adjustment and Well-being*. New Delhi: Discovery Publishing House. ISBN 81-8356-204-3.

Prasanth Kumar, J., Author and Digumarti Bhaskara Rao, Editor (1998). *Effectiveness of Distance Education System*. New Delhi : Discovery Publishing House. ISBN 81-7141-437-0.

Prasanth Kumar, J., Author and Digumarti Bhaskara Rao, Editor (2004). *Methods of Teaching Civics*. New Delhi : Discovery Publishing House. ISBN 81-7141-806-6.

Prasanth Kumar, J., Author and G. Sundara Rao and Digumarti Bhaskara Rao, Editors (2000). *Open University Student Support Services*. New Delhi : Discovery Publishing House. ISBN 81-7141-550-4.

Raja Kumari, M.A. and D.R.S. Sundari, Authors and Digumarti Bhaskara Rao, Editor (2004). *Special Education*. New Delhi : Discovery Publishing House. ISBN 81-7141-846-5.

Raja Kumari, M.A. and D.R.S. Sundari, Authors and Digumarti Bhaskara Rao, Editor (2004). *Methods of Teaching Educational Psychology*. New Delhi : Discovery Publishing House. ISBN 81-7141-820-1.

Rama Krishna Prasad and P. Vide Sagar, Authors and Digumarti Bhaskara Rao, Editor (2004). *Methods of Teaching Physical Education*. New Delhi: Discovery Publishing House.

Rama Krishnaiah, D., Author and Digumarti Bhaskara Rao, Editor (1998). *Job Satisfaction of College Teachers*. New Delhi : Discovery Publishing House. ISBN 81-7141-438-9.

Rama Kumar Ratnam, M.V., Author and Digumarti Bhaskara Rao, Editor (1998). *Dukkha : Suffering in Early Buddhism*. New Delhi: Discovery Publishing House. ISBN 81-7141-653-5.

Rama Seshaiah, P. Author and Digumarti Bhaskara Rao, Editor (2004). *Methods of Teaching Home Science*. New Delhi : Discovery Publishing House. ISBN 81-7141-916-X.

Rama Swamy, K., Author and Digumarti Bhaskara Rao, Editor (2007). *Techniques of Teaching Environmental Science*. New Delhi : Sonali Publications. ISBN 81-8411-035-9.

Ramatulasamma, K., Author and Digumarti Bhaskara Rao, Editor (2002). *Job Satisfaction of Teacher Educators.* New Delhi : Discovery Publishing House. ISBN 81-7141-655-1.

Ramesh, A.R., Author and Digumarti Bhaskara Rao, Editor (2006). *Techniques of Teaching Commerce.* New Delhi : Sonali Publications. ISBN 81-8411-043-X.

Ramesh, Ghanta and Digumarti Bhaskara Rao, Editors (1998). *Environmental Education : Problems and Prospects.* New Delhi: Discovery Publishing House. ISBN 81-7141-423-0.

Ranga Rao, B., Author and Digumarti Bhaskara Rao, Editor (2007). *Techniques of Teaching Economics.* New Delhi : Sonali Publications. ISBN 81-8411-056-1.

Ranga Rao, R., Author and Digumarti Bhaskara Rao, Editor (2004). *Methods of Teacher Teaching.* New Delhi : Discovery Publishing House. ISBN 81-7141-812-0.

Rani, S.S., Author and Digumarti Bhaskara Rao, Editor (2006). *Techniques of Teaching Botany.* New Delhi : Discovery Publishing House. ISBN 81-8411-037-5.

Rathaiah, Lavu and Digumarti Bhaskara Rao (1997). *Achievement Correlates.* New Delhi: Discovery Publishing House. ISBN 81-7141-385-4.

Rathaiah, Lavu and Digumarti Bhaskara Rao, Editors (1996), *International Innovations in Education.* New Delhi : Discovery Publishing House. ISBN 81-7141-359-5.

Ravi Krishna, M., Author and Digumarti Bhaskara Rao, Editor (2004). *Examination System.* New Delhi : Discovery Publishing House. ISBN 81-7141-824-4.

Ravi Kumar, M., Author and Digumarti Bhaskara Rao, Editor (2004). *Methods of Teaching Computer Science.* New Delhi : Discovery Publishing House. ISBN 81-7141-823-6.

Rudramamba, B. and V. Lakshmi Kumari, Authors and Digumarti Bhaskara Rao, Editor (2004). *Methods of Teaching Economics.* New Delhi : Discovery Publishing House. ISBN 81-7141-900-3.

Rudramamba, B., Author and Digumarti Bhaskara Rao, Editor (2003). *Problems of Teaching.* New Delhi : APH Publishing Corporation. ISBN 81-7648-462-8.

Sambasiva Rao, P., Author and Digumarti Bhaskara Rao, Editor (2007). *Techniques of Teaching Psychology.* New Delhi : Sonali Publications. ISBN 81-8411-040-5.

Sanjeeva Rao, P.C., Author and Digumarti Bhaskara Rao, Editor (1996). *A Text Book of Geology.* New Delhi : Discovery Publishing House. ISBN 81-7141-313-7.

Santhanam, T., B. Prasad Babu and S. Sugandhi, Authors and Digumarti Bhaskara Rao, Editor (2007). *Children with Learning Disabilities.* New Delhi : Sonali Publications. ISBN 81-8411-077-4.

Santhanam, T., B. Prasad Babu and S. Sugandhi, Authors and Digumarti Bhaskara Rao, Editor (2008). *Learning Disabilities and Remedial Programmes.* New Delhi : Discovery Publishing House.

Sarala, M.M.O., Author and Digumarti Bhaskara Rao, Editor (2006). *Techniques of Teaching English.* New Delhi : Sonali Publications. ISBN 81-8411-047-2.

Satya Narayana, G., Author and Digumarti Bhaskara Rao, Editor (2008). *Attitude towards Social Studies and Achievement in Social Studies.* New Delhi : Sonali Publications.

Satya Narayana, P.V.V. and G. Krishna, Authors and Digumarti Bhaskara Rao, Editor (2004). *Curriculum Development and Management.* New Delhi : Discovery Publishing House. ISBN 81-7141-813-9.

Satya Narayana, V., Author and Digumarti Bhaskara Rao, Editor (2001). *Physical Education, Social Attitudes and Leadership Qualities.* New Delhi: Discovery Publishing House. ISBN 81-7141-593-8.

Shamsuddin, Sk. and V. Dayakara Reddy, Authors and Digumarti Bhaskara Rao, Editor (2007). *Academic Achievement and Values.* New Delhi : Discovery Publishing House.

Singh, Y.C., Author and Digumarti Bhaskara Rao, Editor (2006). *Techniques of Teaching Science.* New Delhi : Sonali Publications. ISBN 81-8411-041-3.

Sirisha Rani, S., Author and Digumarti Bhaskara Rao, Editor (2007). *Techniques of Teaching Botany.* New Delhi : Sonali Publications. ISBN 81-8411-037-5.

Siva Lakshmi, G.V. and G.L. Subbaiah, Authors and Digumarti Bhaskara Rao, Editor (2004). *Methods of Teaching Environmental Science.* New Delhi: Discovery Publishing House. ISBN 81-7141-839-2.

Sivaratnam Reddy, M., Author and Digumarti Bhaskara Rao, Editor (2004). *Creativity in College Students.* New Delhi : Discovery Publishing House. ISBN 81-7141-697-7.

Srihari, M., Author and Digumarti Bhaskara Rao, Editor (2003). *Values of Prospective Teachers.* New Delhi : Discovery Publishing House. ISBN 81-8356-328-7.

Srinivas Rao, P., Author and Digumarti Bhaskara Rao, Editor (2007). *Principles of Secondary School.* New Delhi : Sonali Publications. ISBN 81-8411-058-8.

Srinivas, G. and Digumarti Bhaskara Rao (2007). *Anxiety of Prospective Teachers.* New Delhi : Sonali Publications. ISBN 81-8411-084-7.

Srinivas, M. and I. Prasada Rao, Authors and Digumarti Bhaskara Rao, Editor (2004). *Methods of Teaching History.* New Delhi : Discovery Publishing House. ISBN 81-7141-803-1.

Srinivasa Rao, Mandalapu, Author and Digumarti Bhaskara Rao, Editor (2003). *Achievement Motivation and Achievement in Mathematics.* New Delhi : Discovery Publishing House. ISBN 81-7141-674-8.

Srinivasulu Reddy, M. and K.R.S. Sambasiva Rao, Authors and Digumarti Bhaskara Rao, Editor (1999). *A Text Book of Aquaculture.* New Delhi : Discovery Publishing House. ISBN 81-7141-482-6.

Subba Rao, K., Author and Digumarti Bhaskara Rao, Editor (2007). *School Education Policy.* New Delhi : Discovery Publishing House. ISBN 81-8356-285-X.

Subba Rao, K., Author and Digumarti Bhaskara Rao, Editor (2007). *Education Planning.* New Delhi : Sonali Publications. ISBN 81-8411-053-7.

Subba Rao, K.P., P. Ayodhya and Digumarti Bhaskara Rao (2004). *Patasala Yajamanyam – Vidhya Vyavasthalu* (School Management and Systems of Education). Guntur : Sri Nagarjuna Publishers.

Sudhakar Reddy, Y., Author and Digumarti Bhaskara Rao, Editor (2003). *Creativity in Adolescents.* New Delhi : Discovery Publishing House. ISBN 81-7141-659-4.

Sudhakar, V., B. Ravindra Babu, D.S. Kumar and Digumarti Bhaskara Rao (2004). *Vidya Sanketika Sastram - Computer Vidhya* (Educational Technology and Computer Education). Guntur : Sri Nagarjuna Publishers.

Suneetha, G., Author and Digumarti Bhaskara Rao, Editor (2004). *Environmental Awareness of School Students.* New Delhi : Sonali Publications. ISBN 81-8411-085-5.

Sunil Kumar, K. and K. Rama Krishana, Authors and Digumarti Bhaskara Rao, Editor (2004). *Methods of Teaching Chemistry.* New Delhi : Discovery Publishing House. ISBN 81-7141-913-5.

Sunita, E. and R. Sambasiva Rao, Authors and Digumarti Bhaskara Rao, Editor (2004). *Methods of Teaching Mathematics.* New Delhi : Discovery Publishing House. ISBN 81-7141-915-1.

Surya Madhava, I., Author and Digumarti Bhaskara Rao, Editor (2006). *Techniques of Teaching Geography.* New Delhi : Discovery Publishing House. ISBN 81-8411-034-0.

Surya Madhava, I., Author and Digumarti Bhaskara Rao, Editor (2007). *Techniques of Teaching Political Science.* New Delhi : Discovery Publishing House. ISBN 81-8411-061-8.

Swamy, K.R., Author and Digumarti Bhaskara Rao, Editor (2006). *Techniques of Teaching Environmental Science.* New Delhi : Discovery Publishing House. ISBN 81-8411-035-9.

Swarna Jyothi, K., Author and Digumarti Bhaskara Rao, Editor (2007). *Educational Research.* New Delhi : Sonali Publications. ISBN 81-8411-063-4.

Swarna Latha, C.D., and Digumarti Bhaskara Rao, Editors (2006). *Encyclopaedia of Biotechnology,* 5 Volumes. New Delhi : Discovery Publishing House. ISBN 81-8356-168-3.

Swarupa Rani, T. and J.R. Priyadarshini, Authors and Digumarti Bhaskara Rao, Editor (2004). *Educational Measurement and Evaluation.* New Delhi: Discovery Publishing House. ISBN 81-7141-859-7.

Valeri V. Koustiouk, Author and Digumarti Bhaskara Rao, Editor (2002). *A Text Book of Cryogenics.* New Delhi : Discovery Publishing House. ISBN 81-7141-642-X.

Vamsi Krishna, V., Author and Digumarti Bhaskara Rao, Editor (2004). *School Psychology.* New Delhi: Discovery Publishing House. ISBN 81-7141-880-5.

Vanaja, M. and N. Sneha Latha, Authors and Digumarti Bhaskara Rao, Editor (2004). *Student Shyness.* New Delhi : APH Publishing Corporation.

Vanaja, M., Author and Digumarti Bhaskara Rao, Editor (1999). *Inquiry Training Model.* New Delhi : Discovery Publishing House. ISBN 81-7141-515-6.

Vanaja, M., Author and Digumarti Bhaskara Rao, Editor (2004). *Methods of Teaching Physics.* New Delhi : Discovery Publishing House. ISBN 81-7141-867-8

Veena Kumari, Balusu and Digumarti Bhaskara Rao (1996). *Operation Black Board.* New Delhi : APH Publishing Corporation. ISBN 81-7024-711-X.

Veena Kumari, Balusu, Author and Digumarti Bhaskara Rao, Editor (2004). *Methods of Teaching Social Studies.* New Delhi : Discovery Publishing House. ISBN 81-7141-899-6.

Veena Kumari, Balusu, Author and Digumarti Bhaskara Rao, Editor (2000). *Psycho-Social Correlates of Achievement.* New Delhi : Discovery Publishing House. ISBN 81-7141-547-4.

Venkata Rao, B., Author and Digumarti Bhaskara Rao, Editor (2007). *Techniques of Teaching Chemistry.* New Delhi : Sonali Publications. ISBN 81-8411-057-X.

Venkata Rao, P. and Digumarti Bhaskara Rao (1989). *A Text Book of Zoology – Junior Intermediate.* Guntur : Vignan Publishers.

Venkata Rao, P. and Digumarti Bhaskara Rao (1989). *A Text Book of Zoology – Senior Intermediate.* Guntur : Vignan Publishers.

Venkateswara Rao, V., Author and Digumarti Bhaskara Rao, Editor (2004). *Problems of Education.* New Delhi : Discovery Publishing House. ISBN 81-7141-841-4.

Venkateswara Rao, V., V. Vijaya Lakshmi and V. Vamsi Krishna, Authors and Digumarti Bhaskara Rao, Editor (2004). *Education For All.* New Delhi : Sonali Publications. ISBN 81-88836-30-3.

Venkateswara Rao, V., V. Vijaya Lakshmi and V. Vamsi Krishna, Authors and Digumarti Bhaskara Rao, Editor (2004). *Education in India.* New Delhi : Sonali Publications. ISBN 81-88836-858-9.

Venkateswara Reddy, L. and Narayana, M. L, Authors and Digumarti Bhaskara Rao, Editor (2004). *Methods of Teaching Rural Sociology.* New Delhi : Discovery Publishing House. ISBN 81-7141-811-2.

Venkateswara Reddy, L. and Narayana, M. L., Authors and Digumarti Bhaskara Rao, Editor (2004). *Education for Dalits.* New Delhi : Discovery Publishing House. ISBN 81-7141-872-4.

Venkateswarlu, K. and S.J. Basha, Authors and Digumarti Bhaskara Rao, Editor (2004). *Methods of Teaching Commerce.* New Delhi : Discovery Publishing House. ISBN 81-7141-808-2.

Venugopala Rao, K., Author and Digumarti Bhaskara Rao, Editor (2000). *Teacher Morale in Secondary Schools.* New Delhi : Discovery Publishing House. ISBN 81-7141-551-2.

Venugopala Rao, K., Author and Digumarti Bhaskara Rao, Editor (2007). *Techniques of Teaching history.* New Delhi : Sonali Publications. ISBN 81-8411-059-6.

Vidya, C., Author and Digumarti Bhaskara Rao, Editor (1996). *A Text Book of Nutrition.* New Delhi : Discovery Publishing House. ISBN 81-7141-309-9.

Vijaya Bharathi, D., Author and Digumarti Bhaskara Rao, Editor (2000). *Educational Philosophies of Swami Vivekananda and John Dewey.* New Delhi : APH Publishing House. ISBN 81-7648-309-9.

Vijaya Bharathi, D., Author and Digumarti Bhaskara Rao, Editor (2005). *Educational Philosophy of John Dewey.* New Delhi : Discovery Publishing House. ISBN 81-8356-024-5.

Vijaya Bharathi, D., Author and Digumarti Bhaskara Rao, Editor (2005). *Educational Philosophy of Swami Vivekananda.* New Delhi : Discovery Publishing House. ISBN 81-8356-023-7.

Vijaya Kumar, S.J., Author and Digumarti Bhaskara Rao, Editor (2006). *Techniques of Teaching Mathematics.* New Delhi : Sonali Publications. ISBN 81-8411-039-1.

Vijaya Lakshmi, D., Author and Digumarti Bhaskara Rao, Editor (2004) *Basic Education.* New Delhi : Discovery Publishing House. ISBN 81-7141-881-3.

Vijaya Lakshmi, V., Author and Digumarti Bhaskara Rao, Editor (2006). *Techniques of Teaching Music.* New Delhi : Discovery Publishing House. ISBN 81-8411-038-3.

Vimala, T.D., B. Prasad Babu and Digumarti Bhaskara Rao, Editors (2007). *Stress, Coping and Management.* New Delhi : Sonali Publications. ISBN 81-8411-086-3.

Visalakshi, V., Author and Digumarti Bhaskara Rao, Editor (2006). *Techniques of Teaching Biology.* New Delhi : Sonali Publications. ISBN 81-8411-045-6.

Visalakshi, V., Author and Digumarti Bhaskara Rao, Editor (2007). *Techniques of Teaching Zoology.* New Delhi : Sonali Publications. ISBN 81-8411-055-3.

Index

A

Accuracy, 194

Achievement in science, 88

American Association for the Advancement of Science, 11, 156

Amphibians, 119

Anecdotal records, 194

Application of metacognition, 39

Aquarium, 30

Arthropods, 152

Assessing in science using teacher observation, 117-122
- methods of assessment, 117-122

Assessment of student achievement in science, 87-92
- criteria for successful teaching in science, 91-92
- evaluating student achievement in science, 88
- mandated tests and reading subject-matter, 88-91

Association for Supervision and Curriculum Development (ASCD), 65, 85

Audio-visual aids, 219

B

Background information, 25

Basal textbooks, 25, 193

Big Book, 90

Birds, 119

Birds of Prey, 95

C

Cenozoic Era, 64

Changing and Sustainable Surface of the Earth, 171

Changing Surface of the Earth, 16, 18, 155

Charts, 208

Children literature and science curriculum, 154-158
- children literature and science, 154-157
- communicating with parents, 157-158

Cicero, 136

Clarity, 136

Collaboration, 27

Comprehension, 158

Computer Assisted Instruction (CAI), 35

Constructivism and science curriculum, 63-72
- constructivist teacher, 63-64
- learning community, 64-68
- reflective teaching, 70-72

two schools of thought pertaining to constructivism, 68-70

Curiosity, 200

Current events in ongoing science lessons and units of study, 14-17

learning opportunities, 15-17

Curriculum development in science, 24-26

D

Data driven decision-making in science, 209-215

decision-making in the curriculum, 210-214

Decision making, 6

Decision-making in science curriculum, 190-195

Deliberation is necessary, 192

Democracy, 14

Developing student interest in science, 73-78

metacognition in the science curriculum, 73-74

scaffolding pupil learning in science, 76-78

self-efficacy and the teacher, 74-76

Dewey, John, 172

Diagnosis, 119, 197

Digital camera, 54

Diverse teaching, 42

E

Earthquakes, 46

Earthworms, 152

Ediger, 2, 9, 44, 19, 222

Edison, Thomas, 60

Encouragement, 76

English Language Learners (ELL), 29

Enjoyment, 27

Erosion, 19, 59

Establishing meaning in science curriculum, 79-86

critical and creative thinking, 82-84

learning opportunities to achieve objectives, 79-82

self-efficacy in the science curriculum, 84-85

Evaporation, 30

F

Fish, 119

Floods, 19

Forest fires, 16

Freedom, 198

Frogs, 11

G

Gill, 161

Growth and development, 93

H

Haiku, 60

Hail, 59

Harassment, 198

Hurricanes and tornados, 16

I

Integrated science curriculum, 148-153

science and the integration of subject-matter, 148-150

separate subjects discipline and

committee endeavors, 150-153

K

Kinds of birds, 205

L

Leadership in science curriculum, 23-28

curriculum development in science, 24-26

library books to expand science learnings, 26-27

skills for science teachers and inservice education, 27-28

Leadership to improve science curriculum, 175-181

efforts toward improving the science curriculum, 176-179

psychology of teaching science, 179-180

Learning opportunities, 15-17

Library books, 26-27

Library, 6

Literacy, 55

M

Mammals, 119, 205

Meaning in science curriculum, 8-13

current events in science units and lessons, 12-13

meaning, teaching, and learning in science, 8-12

Mechta, 24

Mentoring and science teacher, 107-112

evaluation of achievement, 111-112

higher levels of cognition, 110-111

science teacher in the mentoring process, 108-110

Mesozoic Era, 64, 191

Metacognition, 39, 73-74

Methods of assessment, 117-122

Methods of teaching science, 35-40

Methods of teaching science: student and the teaching of science, 35-39

Modern appliances, 52

Motivating student learning in science, 93-99

motivation in science, 94-98

Motivating students in science curriculum, 203-208

factors involved in motivating pupils, 203-208

Motivation, 183, 208

Mudslides, 16

N

National Association of Elementary School Principals, 65

National Research Center, 1996, 162

National Research Council, 12, 19, 26, 114, 180

National Science Education Standards, 1996, 4, 118, 188

National Science Teachers Association (NSTA), 84, 21, 53, 146, 212

Natural disasters, 14, 96

Natural environment, 14

New science teacher in school setting, 100-106

mentoring and the new science teacher, 100-104

new teacher in the instructional arena, 104-105
Newspapers, 194
No Child Left Behind Law, 65
Noddings, 101
Novelty and uniqueness, 173
NSTA Reports, 2009, 183

O

Oral communication in science lessons and units of study, 134-141
discussions in science, 138-140
purposes in communication in science, 136-138

P

Paleozoic Era, 64
Parent/teacher conferences and science curriculum, 52-56
inquiry learning, 55
key structural content in science subject matter, 55
objectivity, 55
problem solving, 55
use of science equipment, 55
Pearson Product Moment, 211
Periodic table of elements, 83
Pitch of words, 145
Plethora of factors, 203
Plethora of interest, 218
Plethora of interesting experiences, 140
Plethora of ways, 185
Poetry in science curriculum, 57-62
motivation to write poetry, 58-60
syllabication and poetry in science, 60-61
Poetry, 57, 206
Portfolios in science, 123-127
philosophy of portfolio use, 123-125
testing to notice student progress in science, 125-126
Pre-student teaching field experiences, 164-169
early field experiences, 164-167
evaluation of pupil progress, 168-169
improving observations, 167-168
Problem-solving, 110
Psychology of learning and science curriculum, 196-202
constructivism in the science curriculum, 200-201
learning opportunities to achieve objectives, 196-200
Pupil, writing and science curriculum, 142-147
strategies to use in teaching and learning, 145-146
written communication in science, 142-145

R

Readiness for learning in science, 44-51, 216-223
readiness and the learner, 216-222
readiness and the learner, 44-50
Reading comprehension in science curriculum, 159-163
increasing reading comprehension in science, 159-160
strategies to stress in

teaching, 161-162
Reflective teaching, 70-72
Rejection, 198
Reliability, 211
Remediation, 119
Reptiles, 47, 119, 219
Revisiting the concepts of scope and sequence in science, 18-22
scope in science teaching, 18-20
sequence in science learnings, 20-22
Rhetoric (public speaking), 136

S

Scaffolding, 38
Scaffolded Silent Reading (ScSSR), 129, 130
School principal as science supervisor, 182-189
criteria for school administrators to emphasize, 182-184
evaluation of achievement in science, 187-188
percentiles, 188
reliability, 187
standard deviation, 188
validity, 187
observational visits in classrooms, 184-185
using computer technology in the classroom, 185-187
Science curriculum, 73-74
Science fairs and student, 170-174
criteria for project development, 170-174
Science for all pupils in the school curriculum, 1-7
Science library, 26
Science teacher, 107-112
Science Teachers Association, 65
Scrapbooks, 208
Self-efficacy and the teacher, 74-76
Shrimp and lobster, 151
Soil erosion, 97
Stimulating science vocabulary environment, 128-133
classroom environment, 132
extending student learnings in science, 128-132
Substitute teacher in science, 113-116
additional needs of the subteacher, 115
inservice education and the substitute teacher, 113-115
Sustained Silent Reading (SSR), 129, 130

T

Tapeworms, 151
Teaching of science, 41-43
Teaching science and English language learners, 29-34
teaching English language learners in science, 30-33
Thorndike, E.L., 125
Trivium of the Middle Ages, 135
TV, 15
Tyrannosaurs rex, 120

V

Vygotsky Zone of Proximal Development, 20

W

Winter, 58
Word recognition, 24
Writing skills, 146